D1315794

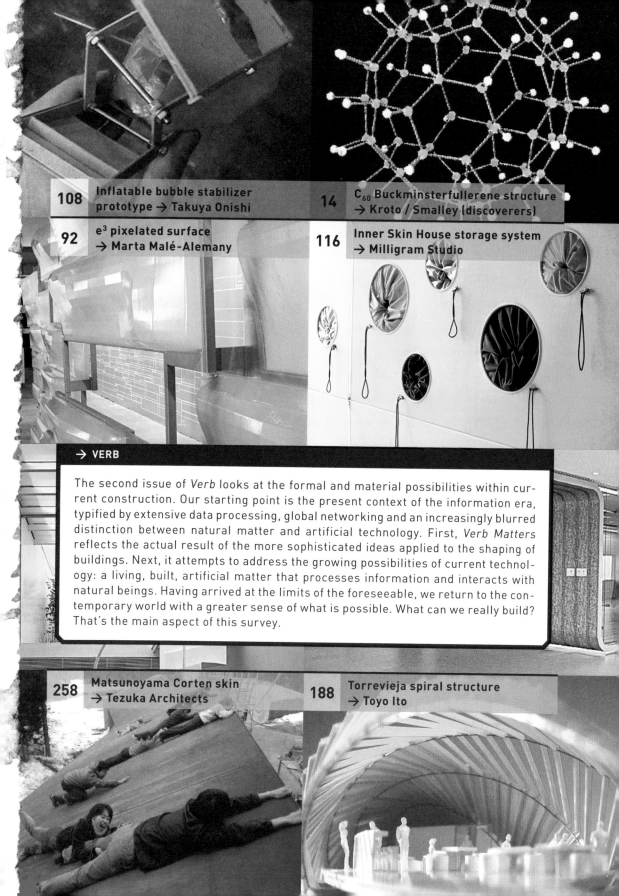

→ VERB

The second issue of *Verb* looks at the formal and material possibilities within current construction. Our starting point is the present context of the information era, typified by extensive data processing, global networking and an increasingly blurred distinction between natural matter and artificial technology. First, *Verb Matters* reflects the actual result of the more sophisticated ideas applied to the shaping of buildings. Next, it attempts to address the growing possibilities of current technology: a living, built, artificial matter that processes information and interacts with natural beings. Having arrived at the limits of the foreseeable, we return to the contemporary world with a greater sense of what is possible. What can we really build? That's the main aspect of this survey.

Norbert Wiener

→ **VERB**

This issue of *Verb* is essentially about networks and matter. As the following "brief history" shows, matter – both organic and inorganic – has the form of networks. Natural systems have the form of networks; human beings are networked organisms who relate by means of networks, and architectures – like humans or computers – are complex networks of matter, energy and information. The history of the 20th century is the progressive discovery of just how much the systems that structure our world – natural and man-made, real and virtual – are nothing less than resilient, intelligent material organizations.

A Brief History
of the Information Age

Michael Kubo, Jaime Salazar

>**1937** Claude Shannon, a young electrical engineering student at MIT, demonstrates in his master's thesis ("A Symbolic Analysis of Switching and Relay Circuits") how the arithmetic used to encode logical operations in mathematics can also be used to describe the behavior of electrical relay circuits. It is a discovery that suggests for the first time how complex systems of electrical signals - digital machines - can be built to replicate the logical operations of human thought.

>**1938-40** R. Buckminster Fuller, a self-taught engineer, works as the science and technology advisor for *Fortune* magazine, where he is responsible for producing articles and graphics on the dynamics of industrial and economic processes like energy production, productivity, expansion of knowledge, and distribution and sharing of world resources.

>**1940** Norbert Wiener, a mathematics professor at MIT, studies the development of automatic range finders for antiaircraft guns together with a young engineer, Julian H. Bigelow. Working to develop "servomechanisms" - devices that can correctly anticipate the trajectory of an airplane by taking into account the elements of past trajectories - Wiener and Bigelow are struck by the seemingly intelligent behavior of these machines, which use "experience" (the results of past and current events) in order to determine future events in real time. They discover that controlling an action with a purpose requires an input of information that forms a "closed loop allowing the evaluation of the effects of one's actions and the adaptation of future conduct based on past performances" - a *feedback loop* in which information on past performance is used to determine current action, which is then re-input as information for subsequent actions.

But Wiener and Bigelow are equally intrigued by a recurring defect in performance, a "disease" of the machine: if too much feedback is input into the servomechanism, the system quickly enters into a series of uncontrollable oscillations. Neurophysiologist Arturo Rosenblueth, a professor at the Harvard Medical School, reveals to Wiener that a similar disease, called the *purpose tremor*, is also found in humans: certain injuries to the cerebellum leave the brain unable to correctly determine muscle responses based on visual input, so that a patient lifting a glass of water to his mouth suffers an uncontrollable amplification of his movements until the water spills on the ground. So the same feedback loop found in the guidance of the antiaircraft gun is equally characteristic of the nervous system, when it orders the muscles to make a movement whose effects are then detected by the senses and fed back to the brain. This connection between control processes in humans and machines immediately leads Wiener, Bigelow and Rosenblueth to generalize their discovery in terms of the human organism, organizing interdisciplinary teams to study living organisms from the viewpoint of servomechanisms engineers and, conversely, considering machine processes with the experience of physiologists.

>**1942** The work of Wiener, Bigelow and Rosenbleuth is first brought to the attention of other specialists at a private meeting in New York organized by the Josiah Macy Foundation. Among the participants is neurologist Warren McCulloch, director of the Neuropathic Institute at the University of Illinois, who has been communicating with Wiener and Bigelow about the mathematical nature of nerve networks in the human brain. Its success in connecting diverse areas of research prompts the Macy Foundation to organize a full series of ten conferences to further expand this emerging field of activity to new disciplines like sociology, political science, psychiatry, anthropology and economics.

>**1943** Wiener, Bigelow and Rosenbleuth's model of control processes in machines and the human nervous system is published for the first time. At the same time, Warren McCulloch and logician Walter Pitts publish the first paper describing the human brain as a *neural network* – a circuit-like system of binary "switches" (nerves) and

J. Robert Oppenheimer   Julian Bigelow   John Von Neumann

© Alan Richards. Courtesy of the Archives of the Institute for Advanced Study, Princeton.

"circuits" (connections) through which instructions and feedback (synaptic transmissions) are sent. They demonstrate that such neural networks are capable of adaptation and self-reorganization, so that when a connection in one part of the brain is severed, its functions switch automatically to another part of the brain.

A. Rosenblueth, N. Wiener and J. Bigelow, "Behavior, Purpose and Teleology," *Philosophy of Science* vol. 10, 1943.
W. McCulloch and W. Pitts, "A Logical Calculus of the Ideas Imminent in Nervous Activity," *Bulletin of Mathematical Biophysics* n. 5, 1943.

>1944 Wiener, Bigelow, McCulloch, Pitts and others form the Teleological Society, an association of scientists in engineering, computers and and neurophysiology, to further explore the relation between "the engineering of control devices" and "the communication and control aspects of the nervous system."

>1945 The debut of ENIAC, the first version of the tool that will allow organized complexity to be approached for the first time: the *electronic digital computer*. Immensely faster than existing mechanical calculators (it can perform an addition in 1/5000 of a second), ENIAC functions based on specific configurations of circuits that have to be manually controlled by switchboard. One of its creators, mathematician John von Neumann, sees the possibility for a general-purpose machine that can be *programmed* to run different tasks, based on instructions stored in a *memory* – the extension of a machine exculsively meant for calculating shell trajectories to a general-purpose machine that can perform tasks closer to the thought processes of the human brain.

J. von Neumann, H. Goldstine, A. W. Burks, "Preliminary Discussion of the Logical Design of an Electronic Computing Instrument", 1946 (www.eecs.harvard.edu/~jonathan/neumann/neumann.html).

ENIAC (Electronic Numerical Integrator and Calculator), 1945. © IBM Germany GmbH.

>1946 After studying improved geometric projections of the Earth's surface onto two-dimensional maps, Buckminster Fuller establishes the Fuller Research Foundation to undertake research on "energetic geometric systems", the geometric principles of physical structures and the flow of energy forces through them.

The year also marks the first in the series of ten Josiah Macy Foundation conferences, chaired by Warren McCulloch. The series quickly establishes itself as one of the primary bridges between the emerging research in biology, neurophysiology and mathematics, technological research on digital computers and communication engineering, and social and behavioral sciences like sociology, political science, anthropology and economics.

Buckminster Fuller with researchers at the Chicago Institute of Design, 1948.
© R. Buckminster Fuller, Courtesy, The Estate of R. Buckminster Fuller.

>1948 The first book by Norbert Wiener gives a name – *cybernetics* – to the emerging, interdisciplinary study of communication and control processes in mechanical and biological systems. Wiener invents the term based on the Greek word *kubernetes* – for "steersman" or "pilot", from which the word governor is also derived – to convey the fundamental idea of control processes as "the art of managing and directing highly complex systems."

Meanwhile, Claude Shannon's paper "A Mathematical Theory of Communication" formally defines the idea of *information* for the first time, and establishes the mathematical principles of how it is communicated, linking the encoding and transmission of information to the principles of energy transfer and entropy in physics and to logical operations in mathematics. In parallel with Wiener's work, Shannon's research inaugurates and provides the mathematical foundations for the new discipline of *information theory.*

Norbert Wiener, *Cybernetics: Control and Communication in the Animal and the Machine* (Cambridge: MIT Press, 1965).
Claude E. Shannon, "A Mathematical Theory of Communication", *Bell Systems Technical Journal*, 1948
(cm.bell-labs.com/cm/ms/what/shannonday/paper.html).

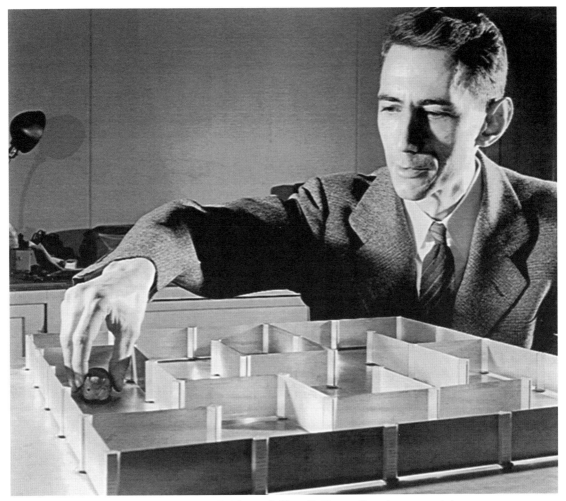

Claude Shannon with *Theseus*, an electromechanical "mouse" able to find its way through a maze and store information on the correct path, 1951. © Lucent Technologies.

Kenneth Snelson,
X-Piece, 1948

>1948 Buckminster Fuller develops his research on energetic geometric structures as a visiting lecturer at Black Mountain College, with students and colleagues like composer John Cage, artist Josef Albers, and dancer Merce Cunningham. Inspired by his lectures, student Kenneth Snelson constructs a sculpture of plywood members and nylon struts whose distribution of continuous tensile stress between suspended compression members leads to the discovery of "multipolar tensional integrity" – the principle of *tensegrity*, where material organizations are considered as networks organized and held in tension by the flow of energy between elements that never touch (like molecular structures or planetary systems), rather than as static and compressive (as in traditional structural analysis). Fuller's fundamental insight into the nature of physical systems points to the development of increasingly weightless, "intelligent" material structures, organized by the dynamic flow of energy and information.

>1951 At Princeton, mathematics student Marvin Minsky builds the first computer simulation of the neural network of synaptic transmissions in the human brain, the SNARC (Stochastic Neural-Analog Reinforcement Computer), whose task is to traverse a maze. It is designed as a randomly wired network through which signals

Buckminster Fuller with tensegrity structures, Southern Illinois University, 1958.
© R. Buckminster Fuller, Courtesy The Estate of R. Buckminster Fuller.

controlling the machine's progress through the maze are sent and received; by reinforcing certain signals based on the computer's performance, the computer gradually improves its rate of success – the first example of a "learning machine."

>**1951** The computer Whirlwind 11, built at MIT, is the first to use a super-fast magnetic memory system, invented by a young electronics engineer from the servomechanisms laboratory, Jay W. Forrester.

>**1953** The encoding of information proves to be one of the fundamental mechanisms of life on earth itself: Biologists James Watson and Francis Crick (originally a physicist) decipher the genetic coding of the DNA double-helix, providing a fundamental link between the processes of material organizations at the molecular scale and those of computers.

>**1954** Expanding the principles of cybernetics to a *general systems theory* that can be applied to social and economic systems, biologist Ludwig von Bertalanffy organizes the interdisciplinary Society for General Systems Research, with mathematicians, biophysicists, sociologists, and economists, among others. By looking at systems (like the human body) in terms of organization and interaction between elements that connect to form a whole – rather than reducing systems to the properties of their individual parts – he reveals that systems "can acquire qualitatively new properties through emergence, resulting in continual evolution," and that "the same concepts and principles of organization underlie the different disciplines (physics, biology, technology, sociology, etc.), providing a basis for their unification."

Ludwig von Bertalanffy, *General Systems Theory: Foundations, Development, Applications* (George Braziller, 1976).

>**1956** Electronics engineer Jay W. Forrester – now a professor at the Sloan School of Management at MIT – founds the System Dynamics Group to study industrial processes as cybernetic systems, governed by multiple feedback loops.
Claude Shannon and two of his students, Marvin Minsky and John McCarthy, sponsor a summer conference at Dartmouth University to discuss the possibility of designing software capable of simulating the processes of human cognition: the inauguration of the field of *artificial intelligence*, based on building computers that can replicate the information processing structures of the human brain.

>**1959** Marvin Minsky and John McCarthy found the Artificial Intelligence Project at MIT to begin the first formal attempts to study the simulation of human thought processes by computers. Two years later, the project becomes the Artificial Intelligence Laboratory.

>**1960-65** The first direct application of cybernetics to architecture: Cedric Price and theatre producer Joan Littlewood propose the Fun Palace, a moveable complex of entertainment and self-education facilities whose design can be changed based on the actual use of the complex. The design consists of a programmed floor surface, vertical trusses supporting auditorium and theater spaces built of moveable walls and floors, and a travelling overhead crane for transporting and assembling parts to form new spaces or dissasemble old ones. The project includes a cybernetic committee run by Gordon Pask, professor at Brunel University; Buckminster Fuller is one of the trustees.

>**1961** A paper by Leonard Kleinrock, "Information Flow in Large Communication Nets," theorizes a new, more efficient method for transmitting messages between points in a network, called *packet-switching*. The system is based on dividing messages into small "packets" of data, sent over connnections that are maintained only for the length of the transmission itself, rather than having to maintain a continuous connection between two points in the network in order for them to communicate. Each packet can take a different path from sender to receiver as lines are blocked or become available, to be reassembled at their destination point; in other words, the flow of information is self-organizing, rather than hierarchical.

>**1962** John Licklider becomes the first director of the Information Processing Techniques Office at ARPA (Advanced Research Projects Agency), a new entity created to fund research in computer and information technology that can lead to major breakthroughs by bypassing standard government research procedures. His goal is to redefine how humans interact with computers, by researching forms of interactive display (the current systems are based on printed numerical input and output), and by designing machines capable of interacting with multiple users at the same time.

>**1964** Engineer Paul Baran, a researcher at the RAND (Research and Development) Corporation, publishes "On Distributed Communications," a study of wartime command and control – specifically the problem of how to build a reliable and resilient network based on unreliable components, and one that can reorganize itself following a nuclear strike. In place of centralized or hierarchical structures, Baran explains the principles of a *distributed network* based on multiple routes between any two points in the system – a structure remarkably similar to the neural networks described by McCulloch and Pitts and the "communication nets" described by Kleinrock. Like Kleinrock, the system would be based on packet-switching: information through the system is automatically rerouted if any channel is cut off, and the redundancy of connections insures that messages are still transmitted effectively even after a significant number of connections are destroyed.

Paul Baran, "On Distributed Communications," series of 11 papers, 1964 (www.rand.org/publications/RM/baran.list.html).

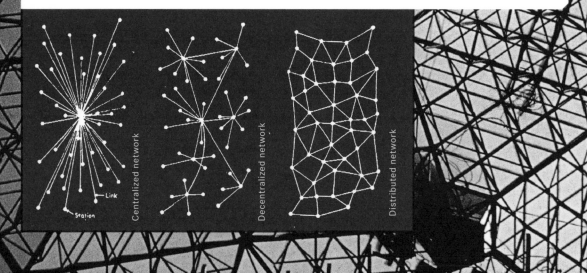

Centralized network

Decentralized network

Distributed network

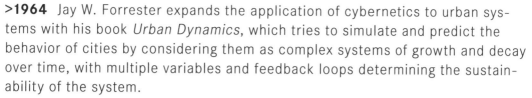

>1964 Jay W. Forrester expands the application of cybernetics to urban systems with his book *Urban Dynamics*, which tries to simulate and predict the behavior of cities by considering them as complex systems of growth and decay over time, with multiple variables and feedback loops determining the sustainability of the system.

>1966 Robert W. Taylor, the third director of the Information Processing Techniques Office at ARPA, proposes building the first network to connect research computers at different locations in the US.

>1967 The US Pavilion of the World's Fair in Montreal is a 75m diameter geodesic dome, designed by Buckminster Fuller together with Shoji Sadao based on the principle of tensegrity. The dome is designed as a very large environmental control system, in which a computer program continuously adjusts the position of triangular sun shades over the surface of the dome based on the location of the sun and the preservation of visual transparency. In this way the dome becomes a distributed network of climate-sensing devices as well as structural forces, an adaptive, "intelligent" skin mediating between interior and exterior. It is also an enormous public success: 11 million people visit the dome over the six months of the Expo.

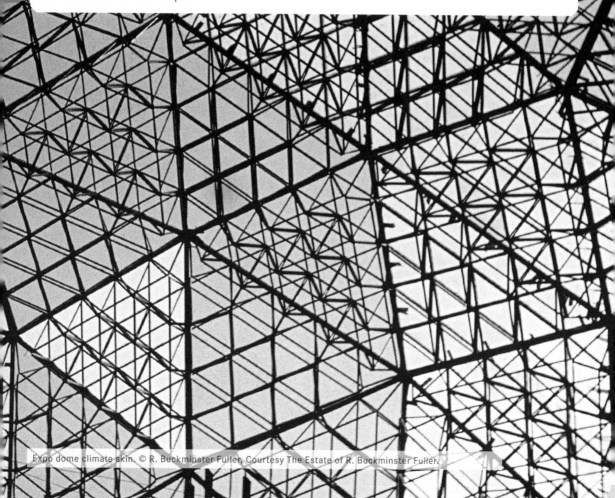

Expo dome climate skin. © R. Buckminster Fuller. Courtesy The Estate of R. Buckminster Fuller.

>**1967** Architect and professor Nicholas P. Negroponte founds the Architecture Machine Group at MIT. He imagines a highly interactive building that would act as a consultant on the question of its own redesign, engaging its owners in an ongoing dialog on issues such as ventilation, illumination and drainage.

>**1968** Inspired by Buckminster Fuller's ideas on understanding the Earth and its processes as whole systems – complex, dynamic networks of interaction and growth - Steward Brand founds the *Whole Earth Catalog*, a mail-order encyclopedia of materials for self-education.

>**1969** The first digital information network, ARPANET, links four universities: the University of California at Los Angeles, Stanford, the University of California at Santa Barbara and the University of Utah. Its architecture, designed by Larry Roberts, is exactly the kind of network theorized by Kleinrock and Baran: a distributed network based on packet-switching, the first realization of such a system in practice.

>**1970** The interdisciplinary group E.A.T. (Experiments in Art and Technology), devoted to exploring the relation between art and science, is comissioned to design the environment for the Pepsi Pavilion at Expo '70 in Osaka, an origami-inspired dome similar to Fuller's geodesic structures. In collaboration with cloud physicist Thomas Mee and meteorologist Yasushi Mitsuta, artist Fujiko Nakaya creates the world's first "fog building": 2520 jet spray nozzles (with a water pressure of 500 psi) and nine pumps surround the pavilion with a pure-water cloud up to 1.8m thick and 46m in diameter.

B. Klüver, J. Martin, B. Rose, eds., *Experiments in Art and Technology: Pavilion* (New York: E. P. Dutton, 1972).

>1971 Jay W. Forrester publishes the third extension of his ideas on system dynamics: *World Dynamics*, which studies the limits of global growth and explores ways of balancing short-term benefit with long-term sustainability in human societies. ARPANET grows to 15 nodes (23 hosts) from the original 4, connecting the east and west coasts of the US for the first time.

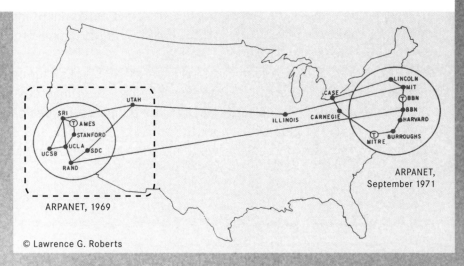

ARPANET, September 1971

ARPANET, 1969

© Lawrence G. Roberts

Fujiko Nakaya's Osaka '70 Pavilion - fogged-in condition, morning, no wind. The air mass of cloud-droplets loses latent heat through evaporation to become cooler than the surrounding air, descending and enveloping the pavilion. © Takeyoshi Tanuma

>1972 Buckminster Fuller implements the first version of the World Game, a massive computer game whose goal is to optimize global living conditions based on data for the distribution of natural resources, energy, population, transport and communication systems. Originally proposed for the US Expo '67 pavilion, the program is based on an interactive world map where theories for resource-sharing and development can be tested and their effects evaluated, a graphical demonstration of world dynamics.

The first basic programs for transmission and management of electronic text messages between users – *email* – are written for the ARPANET: SNGMSG and READMAIL (by Ray Tomlinson of Bolt, Beranek and Newman) and RD (by Larry Roberts at ARPA). The network's designers are surprised to find that sending and receiving email quickly becomes the largest and most important use of the network, a phenomenon that will predict the use of the Internet 20 years later.

>1973 Robert Kahn and Vincent Cerf begin developing an intermediate-level "Inter-networking Architecture" that would allow multiple, independent networks (of diverse design or based on differing technology) to be connected to each other. Called a *transmission control protocol* (TCP), it is the first step in allowing the ARPANET and other specifically-designed networks to be joined together in a flexible, open and widespread network of networks, an "Internet".

>1980 The Department of Defense adopts the TCP/IP (transmission control protocol/internet protocol) standard in order to share in the ARPANET technology base. Within three years, the continued expansion of users leads the network to be split into the MILNET, for military use, and the ARPANET, for research.

>1984 To deal with the dramatic increase in users over ARPANET and similar networks, the Domain Name System replaces the system of numeric email addresses with a system of 7 address categories: .edu, .gov, .com, .mil, .org, .net, and .int. Futurist Kevin Kelly takes over publication of the *Whole Earth Catalog*, renaming it the *Whole Earth Review*. At the same time, Kelly, Stewart Brand (the founder of the Catalog) and Larry Brilliant found the first virtual community of online public computer users, the WELL (Whole Earth eLectronic Link).

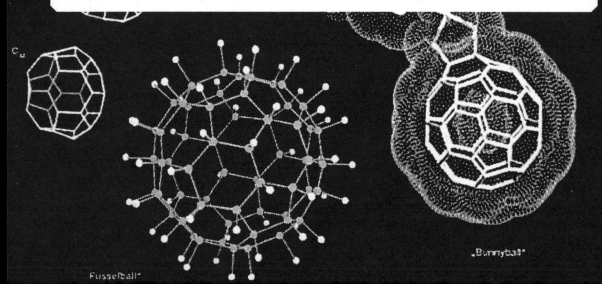

>**1985** Nicholas P. Negroponte and Jerome Weisner co-found the MIT Media Lab. Organic chemists Richard Smalley and Harold Kroto analyze the molecular structure of clusters formed by vaporizing carbon rods using a mass spectrometer. They are suprised to find an unusually large number of clusters containing 60 carbon atoms. This is strange because all of the known types of carbon structures – flat matrices (graphite), 3D lattices (diamond), and unstructured masses (coal) – are infinitely extendible, with nothing to explain why they would have exactly 60 atoms. They find the solution in the geometry of the geodesic dome they had seen at the Montreal Expo 18 years earlier: they realize the clusters must form spherical cages of carbon atoms, with a structure exactly that of a minimal geodesic sphere with 60 nodes (the geometry of a soccer ball). Thus they discover C_{60} – *buckminsterfullerene,* named in honor of their inspiration – the first in a completely new class of closed, cage-like carbon structures called the *fullerenes.* Developing the possibilities of these new cage-like carbon structures leads quickly to the new field of *nanotechnology,* which allows the building of information networks at the molecular scale by transmitting signals chemically (rather than electronically) through microscopic carbon tubes built from fullerenes. The emergence of nanotechnology opens a new field of research into the design of networked, "intelligent" material organizations at the molecular level.

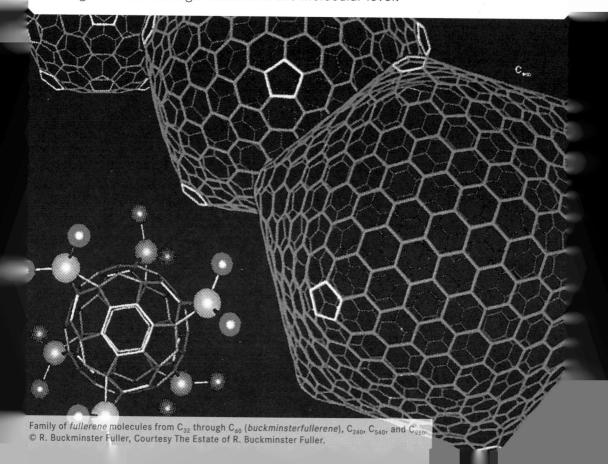

Family of *fullerene* molecules from C_{32} through C_{60} (*buckminsterfullerene*), C_{240}, C_{540}, and C_{960}.
© R. Buckminster Fuller, Courtesy The Estate of R. Buckminster Fuller.

>**1986** Toyo Ito's Tower of Winds, built in Yokohama, Japan, is a first attempt "to convert the environment into information": around an existing ventilation tower, he wraps a 21m high network of perforated aluminum, mirrors, neon rings and lamps that records data from its surroundings, changing its appearance in response to variations in the flow of air and sound – an architectural feedback loop that absorbs aural and physical information and retransmits it as visual information.

>**1990** Tim Berners-Lee, a computer scientist at CERN in Geneva, implements the first *hypertext* system to provide efficient information access to members of the international high-energy physics community. The network already has 300,000 hosts.

>**1992** CERN officially releases the *World Wide Web*. The network grows to 1,136,000 hosts.

>**1993** Mosaic, the first *web browser* that allows the contents of the Internet to be easily searched and accessed, makes the Internet readily accessible to the general public for the first time. The year also marks the first issue of *Wired*, the first magazine devoted to the cultural implications of information and digital technologies. Kevin Kelly is its founding executive editor.

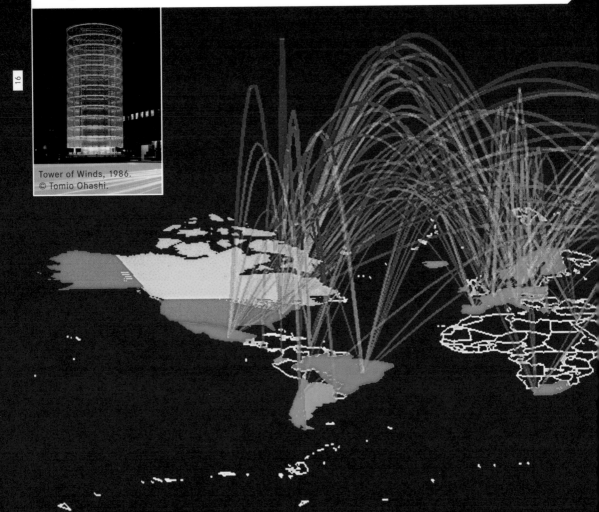

Tower of Winds, 1986.
© Tomio Ohashi.

>**1995** The MIT Media Lab starts the industrial consortium project *Things that Think*. The project aims to imbed computing into common objects around us that are something other than a computer or a telecommunications device, in order to create intelligent, reactive material environments. Neil Gershenfeld, a physics professor at the Media Lab, is asked to lead it.

Kevin Kelly publishes *Out of Control* on the Internet. In it he describes an emerging ecology of machines: future environments where all devices are organisms that are able to react to stimuli and to communicate with other machines and with humans. Kevin Kelly, *Out of Control* (www.kk.org/outofcontrol/).

The Internet has 6,650,000 hosts.

Engineer Mutsuro Sasaki, a frequent structural consultant and collaborator of Toyo Ito, receives a fax with a surprising sketch that looks like algae floating underwater. It is the proposed structure of Ito's competition project for the Sendai Mediatheque: spiral tubes that allow structural forces to flow vertically through the floor plates in parallel with the flow of information through the computer networks that constitute the building's program.

>**1997** Deep Blue, an IBM-designed computer, defeats World Champion Garry Kasparov (3.5 to 2.5) at a 6-game match of chess, the game considered the best test of the progress of computer "intelligence" since the beginnings of digital technology. Originally conceived by John von Neumann and others as an extension of the human brain, the match inaugurates an era in which computer intelligence will increasingly be able to compete directly with that of humans.

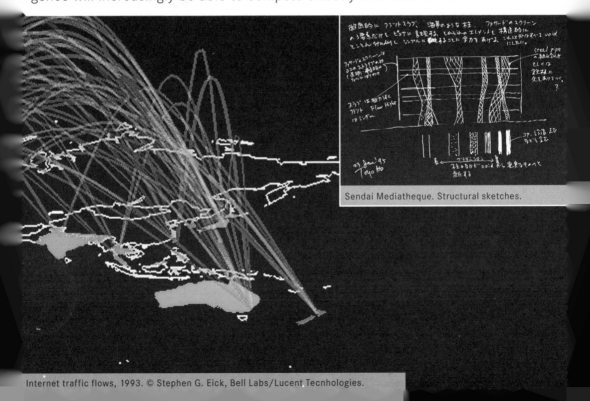

Sendai Mediatheque. Structural sketches.

Internet traffic flows, 1993. © Stephen G. Eick, Bell Labs/Lucent Tecnhologies.

>1998 As part of a team competing for the design of the Swiss Expo '01 site at Yverdon les Bains based on the theme of "Immaterial Design", Diller + Scofidio begin to consider a radical idea: a media pavilion constructed out of "nothing" – that is, out of the elements of the lake in which it stands: air and water. The idea immediately leads their design research in two directions: the material organization of the pavilion's structure, and the design of the air and water cloud that will constitute its visible "architecture." With the help of engineers Passera & Pedretti, the pavilion's structure involves into a suspended tensegrity system; to design the fog cloud, Diller + Scofidio begin collaborating with Fujiko Nakaya (as consultant) and Thomas Mee Industries (as equipment provider), the team responsible for the fog cloud of the Osaka '70 pavilion.

>1999 The Intelligent Room, the first highly embedded, interactive environment, is built by the Artificial Intelligence Lab at MIT.
>2001 The Things that Think research consortium comprises 50 sponsor companies.

This chronology shows the basic idea of *Verb Matters*: the development of learning machines and information networks is the development by the human animal of a new nature, parallel to the nature from which it originates. The Internet is to this "nature" created by man what the biosphere is to the original nature. So ecology is not a return to the natural but a different technological state. This idea is clear in the work of architects like Toyo Ito, but it also explains why the implications of information technology have been best understood by "alternative" thinkers like Kevin Kelly or Buckminster Fuller. Not many people, and fewer architects, know this version of the second half of the twentieth century.

Yverdon les Bains, February 2002

100 m

35 m

25 m

10.85 m

22

Albert Ferré, editor

Dirk Hebel, project architect

Material networks operate at all scales: from the biggest to the smallest. So a build-ing by Fuller is the same as a determinate molecule of carbon, and OMA's designs for Prada (see page 80) are like biological tissues at a large scale. Atoms link to form networks, just like the Internet or tensegrity structures. The solid walls of a building "blur" – they disappear – when observed at an atomic scale. But can a building disappear at full scale as well? Can a building be made out of "nothing"? This is what Diller + Scofidio have done in the Blur Building, a pavilion built for the Swiss Expo in 2002.

Angel Deck

Media platform

Swan

13 m

Fiberglass reinforced plastic (GFK)

Blur building > Diller & Scofidio

Studio Passera & Pedretti, www.ppeng.ch

"A Swiss Italian cloud in Yverdon", Antonio Paronesso > A tensegrity is characterised by the relation between the components forming it and the volume defined by their geometry. Exploiting this particular aspect it is possible to realize interesting and extremely light and transparent architectural solutions based on a new concept of inner space.

According to the definition of R.B. Fuller, a tensegrity system is established when a set of discontinuous compressive components interacts with a system of continuous tensile components to define a stable volume in space. The basic cell invented by Fuller is composed of three non-touching struts connected by nine cables. With this definition it is not possible to have 2 or more struts converging at the same node of the system. Also, to assure overall stability, it is necessary to prestress the cable components so that they will always be in tension under every load case.

To simplify these very demanding requirements of Fuller's definition and to obtain more feasible solutions, we studied a new module for the tensegrity system based on a previous work of B.B. Wang. Our basic cell, called 'bi-pyramidal modulus', is composed by two opposite pyramids sharing the same trapezoidal base. The edges of the trapezium are beams connected by rigid nodes. The vertical strut situated at the centre of the base is stabilised by eight diagonal rods.

Motivated by the positive results of our studies, for the cloud project of the arteplage EXPO.02 in Yverdon, we proposed a tensegrity structure entirely based on our new bi-pyramidal modulus. The project of the cloud above the lake Neuchâtel in Switzerland, conceived by New York architects Diller & Scofidio, offers the visitor a

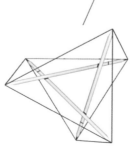
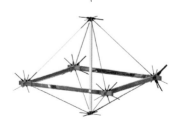

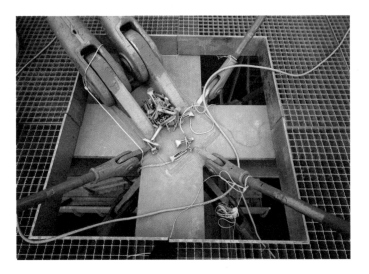

suggestive journey inside a huge artificial cloud produced by the 32,000 nozzles of the fog-system suspended from the tensegrity system.

Only four columns, resting on pile foundations in the water, support the steel structure that has the shape of an ellipse. The dimensions are 60x100m and the maximum height is 23m. The central part among the columns is composed by 4x4 square cells with 10m beams located at a level of 10.85m from the water surface of the lake. The maximum span of the cantilever outside the four columns is 35m. The upper and lower nodes of all the pyramids are connected by two layers (upper and lower) of rods oriented in the same direction as the main axis of the ellipse. The columns are the prolongation of four of the vertical tensegrity struts. The stability of the structure is achieved by connecting the rigid nodes of the cells located around each column to the foundation using four couples of rods. The net of tubes of the fog-system surrounds the entire structure.

The first and main area reserved to the public is situated at level 10.85 and is an elliptical stage with dimensions 48x78m. The second area called the 'Angel Deck' is located on the top of the columns and vertical struts of the central part of the tensegrity at a level 19.20m from the surface of the lake. All the other secondary structures (entrance, exit and emergency stairs, elevator and access ramp, and technical room) are completely isolated from the ground and suspended from the main structure by struts stabilized with bracing rods.

From a static point of view the most interesting feature of the project is the use of the bi-pyramidal model that, thanks to its characteristics, leads to a rigid structure without the need to apply an additional prestress to the system. In fact the field of tensions inside the rods, caused by the shape of the system and by its self-weight, leads to a stiff structure, which is suitable for the purpose of the artificial cloud. The only further work necessary to the rods is the adjustments of those elements that at the end of the assemblage are slack.

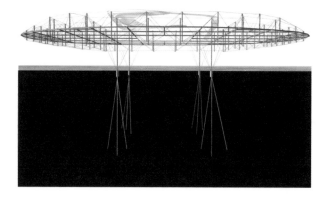

The rods are made of steel with strength properties of F_y = 460 N/mm^2 and F_u=625 N/mm^2.*
The steel of all the other components (struts, nodes etc.) is Fe E 355 C. The beams are HEB 400 in the central part and HEA 400 and HEA 280 in the cantilever part. The columns are steel pipes ROR 508x20 while the vertical struts are ROR 323.9x7.1 and ROR 219.1x6.3.
The upper diagonal rods of the cells of the columns are couples of M72 while the lower ones are couples of M60. All the others rods have a diameter ranging from M30 to M64.
* F_y: yield strength, F_u: ultimate strength

The intricate geometry makes it hard also for experts to understand the way loads applied to the tensegrity are transmitted to the foundations. This complexity is also related to the invisibility, from a distance, of the diagonal rods of the tensegrity, which makes the vertical struts appear like sticks floating in the air.

From an architectural standpoint, the construction is very suggestive. When the fog system is on, people have the sense of being inside a big cloud. When the structure is visible it looks like a huge space ship floating above the lake.

Because of its distance (200 m) from the shore, the structure was mounted by means of cranes operating on a floating pontoon. The central part among the four columns was installed first. During this phase the two columns closer to the shore were stabilized with temporary cables. Then the cantilever part of the structure was assembled, and later all the secondary structures.

To correctly evaluate the stresses in the components of the overall structure, the different phases of the assemblage were considered in the numerical analysis.

In the first phase of the study we computed the displacements produced by the dead load of the tensegrity at the end of the assembly.

In the second phase the results of the first phase were used to formulate the kinematics compatibility between the tensegrity and the Angel Deck, assuming the assembly of the Angel Deck structure in isostatic conditions.

In the third phase the displacements of the Angel Deck structure at the end of the installation were introduced in the formulation of its final constraints, to be used for the analysis of the overall structure under the effect of the external loads.

In the fourth phase, we simulated the length adjustment of those rods that are slack at the end of the mounting. In the last phase the forces applied by the fog system to the rods of the tensegrity are modelled.

More than one hundred load cases were studied combining the wind and snow loads with more than thirty positions of a moving live load of 5 kN/m² over the surface of 100 m², located everywhere on the public areas of the platform and the Angel Deck. In addition, more than twenty load cases associated to the failure of one rod in tension were examined. This study has confirmed the stability of the system under the sudden breaking of a rod and has shown the capability of the structure to maintain an elastic rearrangement of the inner efforts of the components. These positive characteristics are primarily due to the hyperstatic structure generated by the bi-pyramidal tensegrity and to the presence in the system of slack rods that are activated (put in tension) when the failure of one component occurs.

The study and the geometry check of the complicated details of the steel structure were done using the 3D graphic development software "Inventor" by Autodesk.

To increase productivity and shorten the time to verify the geometric compatibility between the different components (rods, stairs etc.) of a very complex structure with secondary structures (often modified by the architects during the design phase), we used computer graphic programs like "Explorer" by Alias/Wavefront and others.

Thanks to the use of the powerful software mentioned above and to the continuous engagement of our colleagues, it was possible to respect the planning of the execution project of a construction continuously updated.

4
21
18
Stair 1b
9
Stai
7
5
Stair 3b
13
4
12
Stair 5
Stair 1a

11.75

1. Sloped entrance ramp (3.3%) of prefabricated FVK sections
2. Flat exit ramp of prefabricated FVK sections
3. Flat exit ramp from emergency stairs of open mesh steel grating
4. Emergency egress stair with prefabricated open mesh steel grating treads
5. Primary entrance stair with prefabricated open mesh steel grating treads
6. Primary exit stair from Angel Deck to exit ramp with prefabricated open mesh steel grating treads
7. Guardrails of rigid clear acrylic panels and steel grabrail or plexi tube with integrated light system
8. Guardrail and handrail steel tube
9. Hydraulic elevator with glass cab and open shaftway
10. Tensegrity system of steel tension rods, ROR columns and steel HEB compression beams
11. Fog nozzles and associated water lines suspended throughout from tensegrity system at 1.2m in any direction (except where spatial conflicts occur)
12. 4 primary support columns for tensegrity structure

13. Electrical room of F60 construction suspended from steel beams above
14. Platform (media platform) of prefabricated open mesh steel grating panels on steel sub-structure
15. LED columns located throughout platform on each side of a vertical stud
16. Stair to Angel Deck of open mesh steel grating
17. Angel Deck of sand coated translucent FVK material
18. Deck material "morphs" into coverings for toilet area and bar concession area
19. Ramp
20. Bar concessions area. Equipment and general storage under countertop
21. Canopy over bar concessions area of FVK material morphed from floor
22. 7 unisex toilets on lower level
23. Frosted glass doors
24. Communal sink recessed into the lip of the bar deck
25. Nozzle free zone
26. Mechanical and electrical feed suspended from underside of exit stair

BLUR BUILDING. YVERDON-LES-BAINS, SWITZERLAND

Architects: Diller + Scofidio. Principals: Elizabeth Diller, Ricardo Scofidio; Project Leader: Dirk Hebel. Project Team: Charles Renfro, Eric Bunge. Client: EXPO 02 by extasia. Structural Engineers: Passera & Pedretti. Sound installation by artist: Christian Marclay. Media: Diller + Scofidio and Ben Rubin, EAR Studio. Media Associate: Mark Wasiuta. Photographs: Ramon Prat, Dirk Hebel. Blur is part of the Arteplage Yverdon-les-Bains for Swiss EXPO 02. In a project collaboration, several architects and artists founded the group "extasia", which won the competiton for the site in Yverdon. See Diller + Scofidio, *Blur: the making of nothing* (NY: Abrams, 2002)

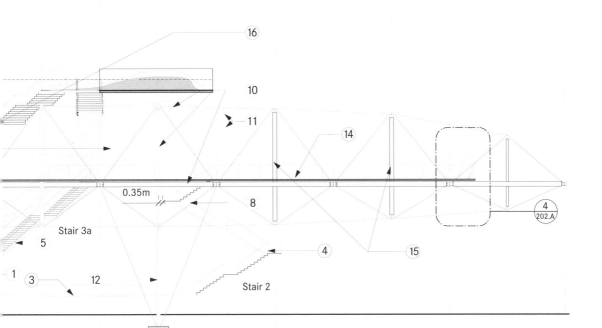

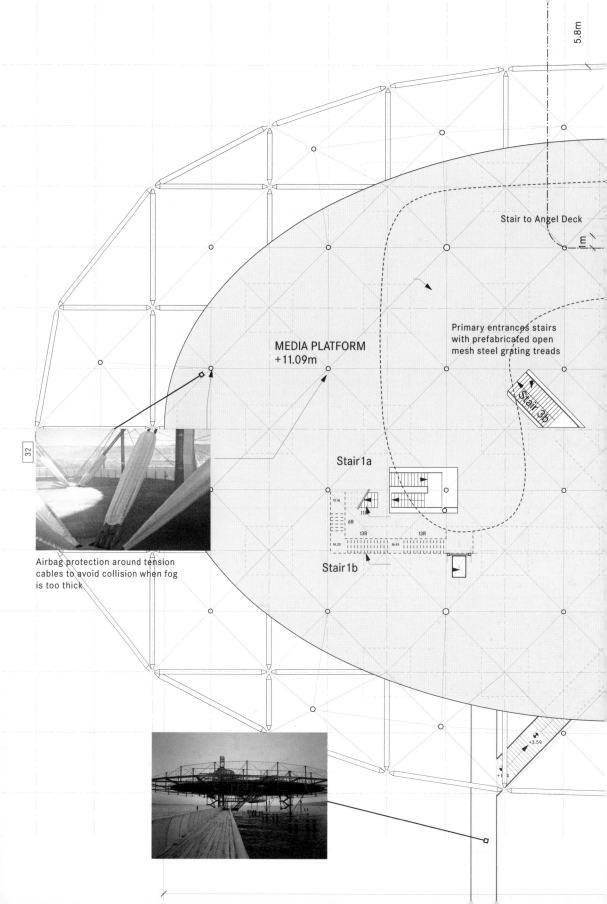

Stair to Angel Deck

m

Primary entrances stairs
with prefabricated open
mesh steel grating treads

MEDIA PLATFORM
+11.09m

Stair 3b

Stair1a

13.16
11
6R
13R   13R
14.20   16.45
Stair1b

32

Airbag protection around tension
cables to avoid collision when fog
is too thick

+3.59

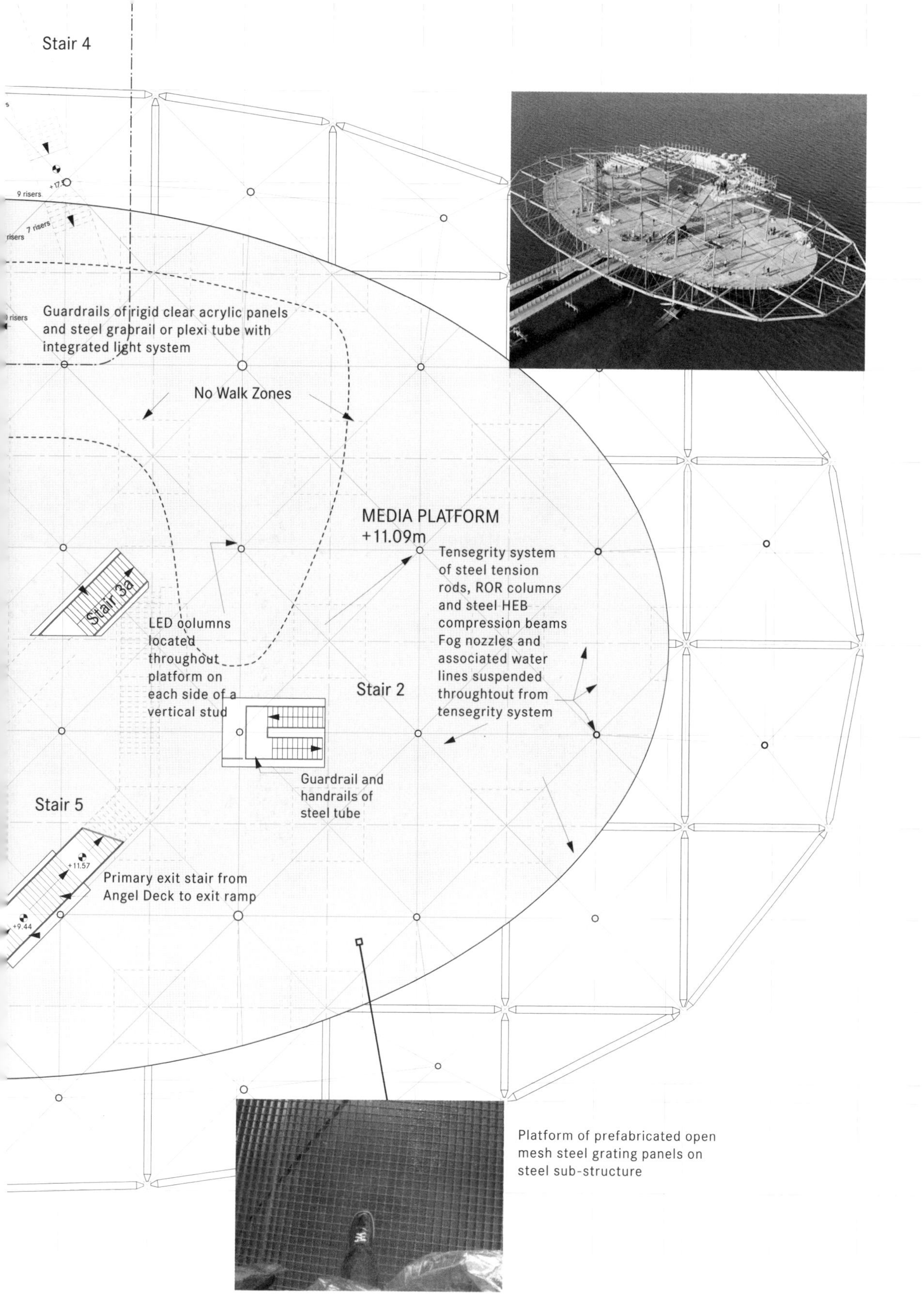

Stair 4

9 risers   +17

7 risers

risers

0 risers

Guardrails of rigid clear acrylic panels
and steel grabrail or plexi tube with
integrated light system

No Walk Zones

MEDIA PLATFORM
+11.09m

Tensegrity system
of steel tension
rods, ROR columns
and steel HEB
compression beams

Stair 3a

LED columns
located
throughout
platform on
each side of a
vertical stud

Fog nozzles and
associated water
lines suspended
throughtout from
tensegrity system

Stair 2

Guardrail and
handrails of
steel tube

Stair 5

+11.57

Primary exit stair from
Angel Deck to exit ramp

+9.44

Platform of prefabricated open
mesh steel grating panels on
steel sub-structure

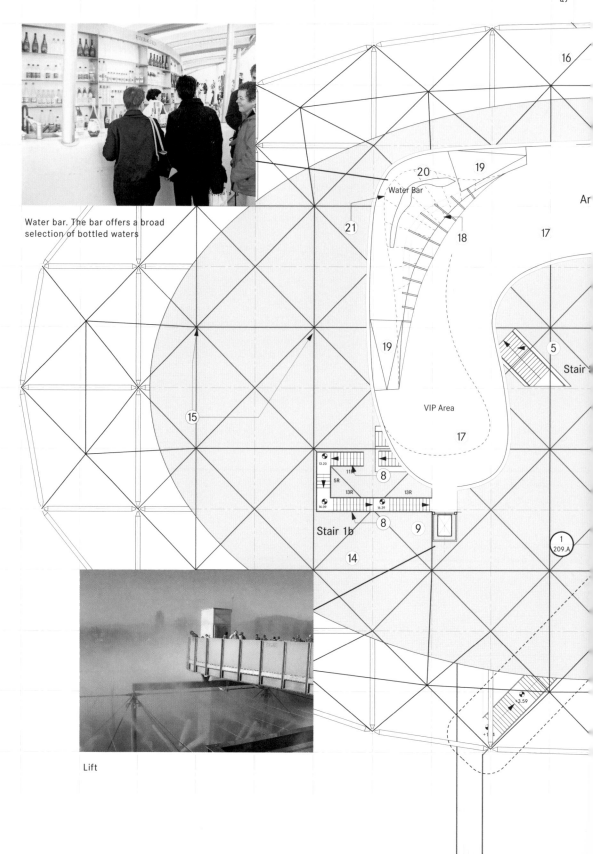

16

19

20

Water Bar

Ar

21

18

17

19

15

5

Stair

VIP Area

17

13.20

11R

8

5R

14.09

13R

13R

16.39

8

Stair 1b

9

1
209.A

14

+3.59

Water bar. The bar offers a broad
selection of bottled waters

Lift

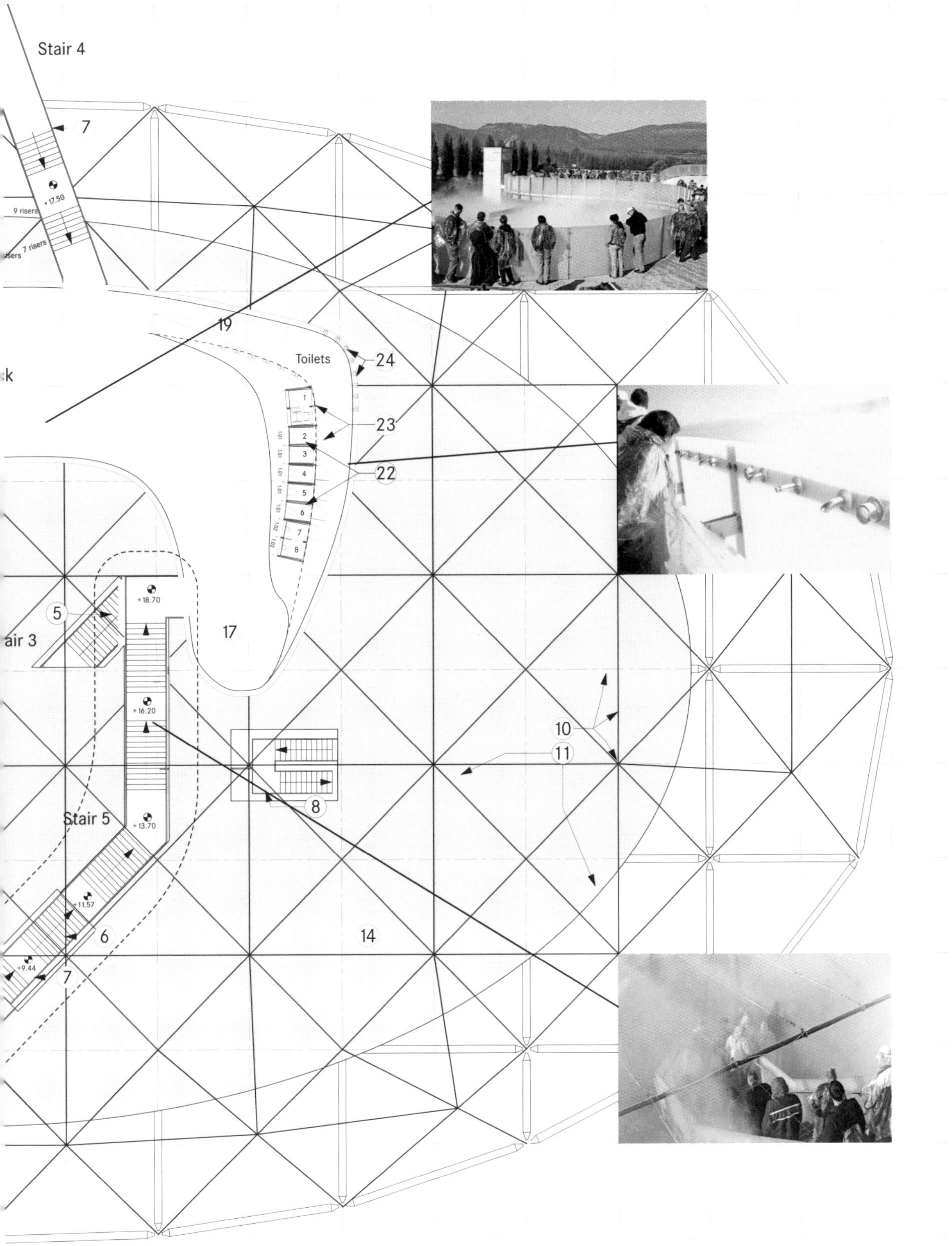

Stair 4

7

9 risers   +17.50

isers 7 risers

19

k

Toilets

24

1

23

2

3

22

4

5

6

7

8

+18.70

5

air 3

17

+16.20

8

Stair 5   +13.70

10

11

+11.57

6

+9.44

7

14

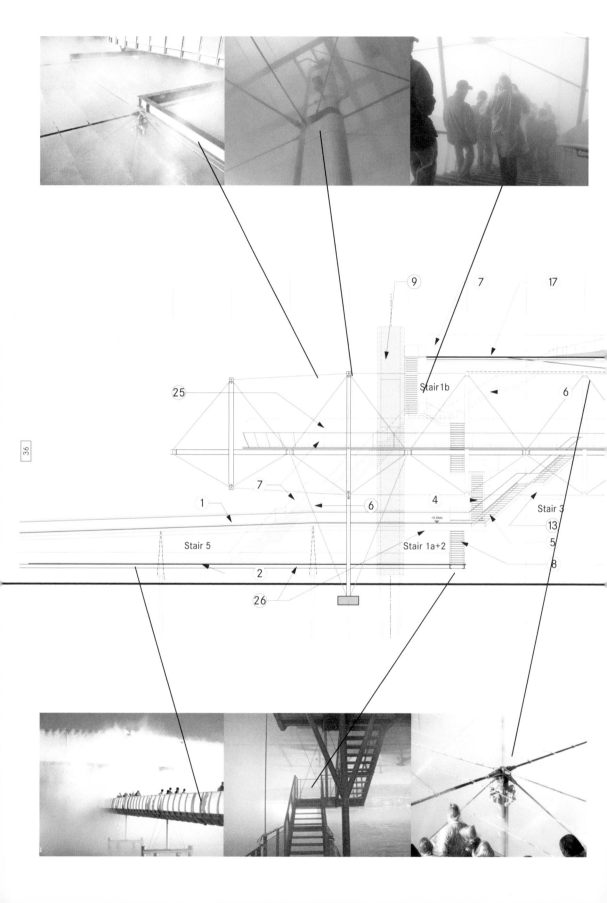

9

7

17

25

Stair 1b

6

7

1

6

4

+5.04m

13

Stair 3

Stair 5

5

Stair 1a+2

8

2

26

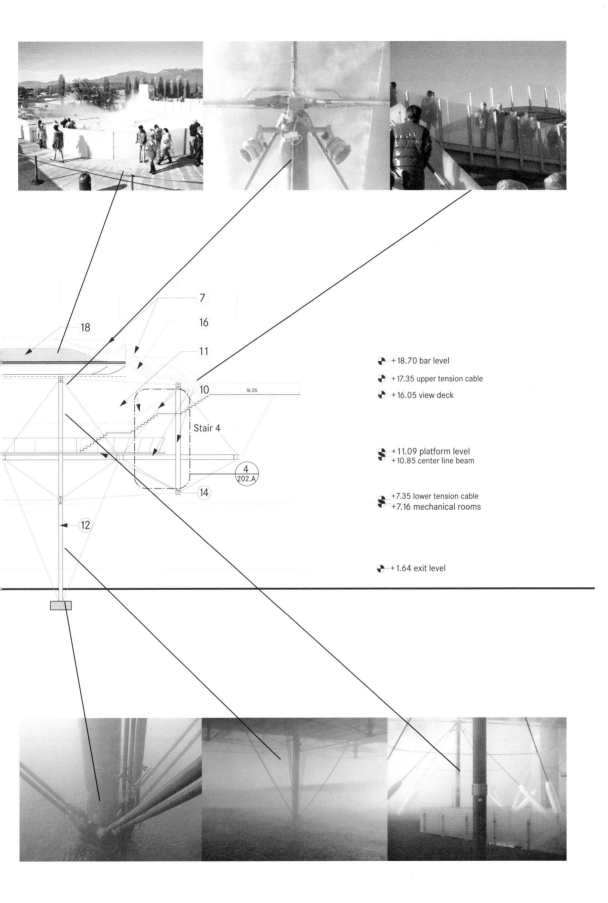

7
16
18
11
10

16.05

Stair 4

4
202.A

14

12

+ 18.70 bar level
+ 17.35 upper tension cable
+ 16.05 view deck

+ 11.09 platform level
+ 10.85 center line beam

+ 7.35 lower tension cable
+ 7.16 mechanical rooms

+ 1.64 exit level

// BLUR EXPERIENCE //

///// 0-15 km/h 75-100% /////

///// 15-30 km/h 50-75% /////

///// 30-45 km/h 25-50% /////

//// BLUR change de forme selon les conditions externes de météorologie. Principalement c'est la vitesse du vent et l'humidité relative de l'air qui déterminent la densité et la transparence du brouillard sur la structure. ////////

/// BLUR aendert seine Gestalt abhaengig von den aeusseren Wettereinfluessen. Vor allem Windgeschwindigkeit und Luftfeuchte entscheiden darueber, wie dicht oder transparent sich der Nebel ueber die Struktur legt. //////////

// BLUR changes aspect according to the external meteorological conditions, which are first the windspeed and the humidity in the air, overdriving the density and the transparency surrounding the structure. ///////////////

High winds reveal the leading edge of the structure and produce long fog trails; high humidity and high temperatures expand the fog outwards; high humidity and cool temperatures make the fog fall to the lake and roll outwards; low humidity and high temperatures have an evaporating effect; air temperature cooler than lake temperature produces a convection current that lifts the fog upwards.

Upon entering the fog mass, visual and acoustic references are erased, leaving only an optical white-out and the white noise of pulsing fog nozzles. Entering Blur is more like stepping into a habitable medium, one that is formless, featureless, depthless, scaleless, massless, surfaceless, and dimensionless. On the platform, movement is unregulated and the public is free to wander in an immersive acoustic environment.

Its primary building material is one indigenous to the site: water, pumped from the lake, filtered and shot as a fine mist through a dense array – every 20 centimeters – of high-pressure mist nozzles. The resulting fog mass changes from season to season, day to day, hour to hour, and minute to minute in a continuous dynamic display of natural versus man-made forces. A smart weather system reads the shifting climactic conditions of temperature, humidity, wind speed, and direction, and processes the data in a central computer that regulates water pressure to an array of 31,500 nozzles.

From the platform, the public can ascend a stair to the Angel Deck at the summit, emerging through the fog as if piercing a cloud layer in flight. From the deck, the public has a panoramic view of Expopark and the lake.

Water is not only the physical context and the dominant architectural material of Blur, it is also a source of culinary pleasure: submerged one half level below the Angel Deck is the Water Bar. The bar offers a broad selection of bottled waters including spring waters, artesian waters, mineral waters, sparkling waters, and distilled waters from around the world that satisfy the most discerning water connoisseur. The public is invited to drink the building.

Inhalating big quantities of oxygen has the effect of making people 'happy'. The fog also gives a feeling of security. There was a woman who visited the building many times; when asked why she came so often, she said she was from Sarajevo, had lived through the war there, and that the only time she felt secure during the war was on foggy days. She came to the building because she felt secure and relieved in the middle of the cloud.

44

5°

27.3 m

48

→ VERB

Like the Blur building, the Scharnhauser Park Town Hall combines the artificial matter of architecture with the natural matter of wind and rain – forces that affect any building, but here are used as the matter of the project itself. So (as we said in the first issue of *Verb*, on page 121), everything is related, and matter – artificial or natural – is not so inert as it seems.

Ostfildern, Stuttgart

38 m

8 m

Scharnhauser Park Town Hall > Jürgen Mayer H.

Planned on the grounds of a former American military barracks vacated in 1992, Scharn-hauser Park is the fifth town in the constellation of suburbs that makes up Ostfildern, located between the city of Stuttgart and its airport and easily serviced by train from Stuttgart's main station. This new town for 10,000 people is formed by a dense combination of housing types with community and commercial facilities for young families and elderly people, over-lapped with a grid-system of green boulevards or linear gardens used as playgrounds and neighborhood parks. Though not at all a traditional, low-rise garden city, the 'Park' is mar-keted as an ecologically-friendly and socially-balanced mid-rise urban scheme.

A few preserved housing wings of the former barracks were the only existing elements of the new town when the international competition for the design of the Town Hall was held in 1998. Following the decentralized concept of Ostfildern's city administration, the brief called for a mixture of traditional town hall functions and public programs – city library, evening school, conference facilities, wedding hall, art gallery, and a new media space – so as to enhance the development of the new community. Given the abstract nature of the town and the community at the competition stage, the project and the subsequent building define and stage within their own limits the interaction of programs and their imagined users, thus functioning as a self-referential piece of the city – a "hyperprogrammed public space", as Jürgen Mayer H. likes to call his building.

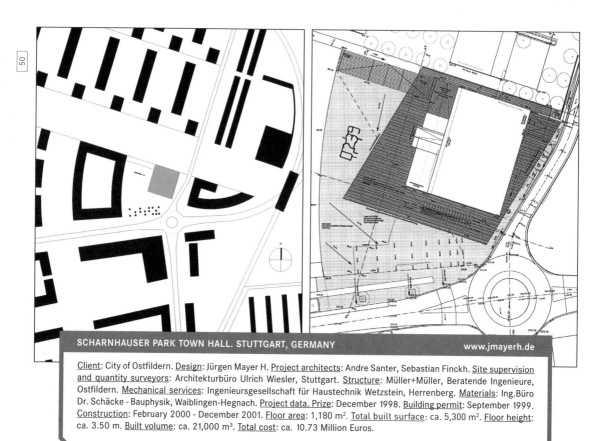

SCHARNHAUSER PARK TOWN HALL. STUTTGART, GERMANY   www.jmayerh.de

Client: City of Ostfildern. Design: Jürgen Mayer H. Project architects: Andre Santer, Sebastian Finckh. Site supervision and quantity surveyors: Architekturbüro Ulrich Wiesler, Stuttgart. Structure: Müller+Müller, Beratende Ingenieure, Ostfildern. Mechanical services: Ingenieursgesellschaft für Haustechnik Wetzstein, Herrenberg. Materials: Ing.Büro Dr. Schäcke - Bauphysik, Waiblingen-Hegnach. Project data. Prize: December 1998. Building permit: September 1999. Construction: February 2000 - December 2001. Floor area: 1,180 m². Total built surface: ca. 5,300 m². Floor height: ca. 3.50 m. Built volume: ca. 21,000 m³. Total cost: ca. 10.73 Million Euros.

Jurgen Mayer H. This is intended to be a service building for the residents of this new town, rather than an institution - a new form of community center which is referred to these days as a ¨transparent¨ town hall, where you can have internet spaces, a library with magazines, concerts...

This was originally supposed to be a 24-hour open building, accessible from all different sides. But the idea changed a lot from the competition stage to realization.

Originally two more entrances were planned, one from the garage and the other one from the upper garden level. But the more we worked on the project the more problematic it became to the city in terms of security. In the end we have just one big entrance, with a small back entrance for people who work in the building and next to it the entrance to the parking garage, which will be built under the square on the other side of the building.

On the exterior, the use of double-glazing was a way to achieve a clear-cut definition of the façade, while simultaneously providing an efficient climatic control system. The building has no air-conditioning, and the only way to guarantee temperature control in the summer time was by means of this ventilated façade, which keeps interior daytime temperatures cool enough and allows the concrete ceilings to cool down at night. All of the green interior walls are drywall construction, but they were initially thought of as glass partitions. There were two issues that forced us to close them off. One was fire protection, as it became too expensive to have fire-resistant glass walls. The other issue was privacy, both for the people who work here and for those who come here to consult on conflictive social, economic or legal situations. The green color also refers back to the original idea of a glass wall with a natural green stain.

Verb The most prominent and public activating features of the project are the leaking cantilevered roof which forms the characterizing feature of the main façade, and the massive poles on the adjacent square with thin light-strings that swing in the wind. The fact that this new town markets itself as ecologically friendly became a justification for water collection and the rain-screen, but this is not the type of building which, as the main public piece of the new town, seems to most directly represent this policy.

JM This is an argument that came later, as a justification before the city administration. But it's interesting to look at the different layers from which this issue is approached, depending on whom you talk to. If you circumscribe it to a critical architectural discussion, it would be like rethinking the leaking modernist roof and turning it around to make something productive out of it. There is also the symbolic layer of how a roof, which is intended for protection, suddenly challenges your access to the building because you are forced to walk through the rain. But more simply, climate is the most common topic of conversation, and so the artificial rain is something people can always talk about and bring their visitors and guests to

come and see. So dealing with weather and making the building climate-responsive is also an efficient strategy to foster the development of all sorts of communication.

Verb Beyond their specific effects on the daily life of the new inhabitants of the building and the surrounding town, these activators are also indicators of the possibilities of technological implementation in buildings, and of the inevitable association between technology and nature.

JM In fact, if the roof can be seen as nature animated by computers, since it's a computer-generated rain, then the poles with the wind-lights (which define the exact volume missing under the cantilevered roof) stand for technology animated by nature, because the wind moves them around. Each of the 16 poles houses a web-cam focused on the spot of pavement located vertically under the light-strings, tracing their wind-animated movement and broadcasting it to the city's public website as an animated grid of light-points. You have public art in real public space, and virtual art in virtual public space.

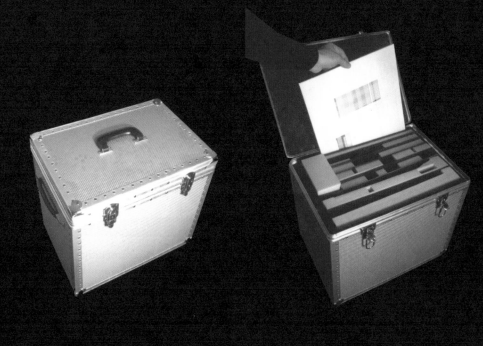

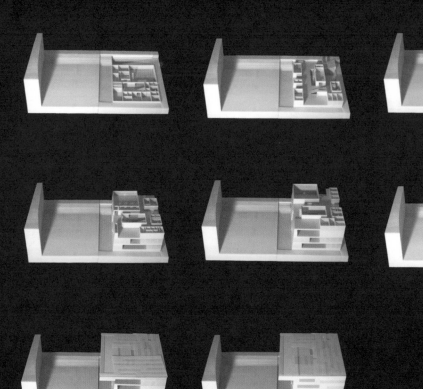

Jürgen Mayer presented the Stadthaus competition entry to the city council through two apparently opposing but fundamentally complementary models: the *alubox* and the *e.gram*. The alubox is a heavy aluminum case containing a set of styrofoam trays, each representing the organization of one floor of the building. The e.gram is a small glass cube containing a three-dimensional laser delineation of the structural and programmatic cores and connecting vertical voids that run through the building, relating spaces and functions. The box suggests the compactness of the volume; the contained layers of trays reveal its complex spatial organization, while the glass cube shows the fluidity or transparency of this organization.

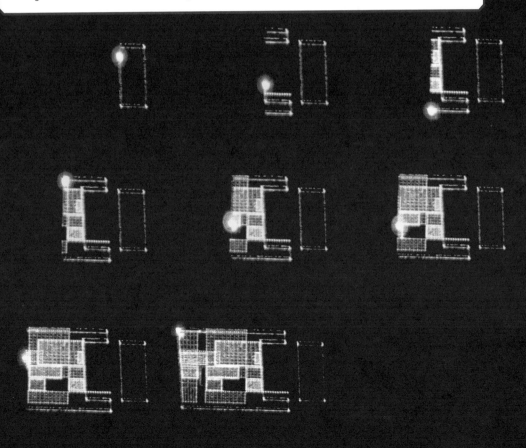

BUILDING ORGANIZATION The Town Hall consists of a distinct architectural volume whose perimeter measures 38m x 27.3 m, and whose contours delimit the site. This volume is canted at an angle of 5° along its east-west axis, while the various levels and the roof remain horizontal. The result is a rhomboidal cross-section. On the side abutting the market square, a canopy-style overhanging roof juts out 8 meters along the entire length of the building. From this canopy, water from the Zeitbrunnen (or "Time Fountain") trickles down into a pool of water lying below. A footbridge crosses the water to lead into the Town Hall from the market square. Viewed topologically, the Town Hall consists of four levels; these are partially cut out to make air spaces and vistas possible. The spatial design within follows the principles of envelope-core and mass-indentation. Individual cores assume functions which are accommodated in isolation from one another. The remaining functions are designed to be open and transparent. The building is thus divided into variegated brighter and darker areas. Around these cores, the structure's envelope lies like a band, tying individual "blocks" together. Indentations into the total volume create a fusion of interior and exterior spaces. Thanks to this system, complex functional interconnections can be organised without difficulty. A central light shaft and stairway serves as a point of orientation.

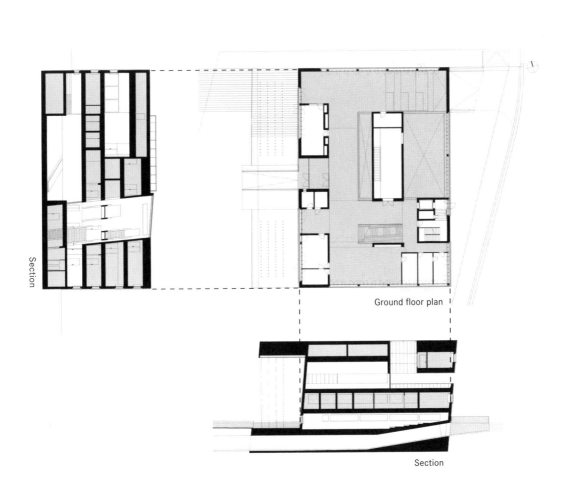

Section

Ground floor plan

Section

The Town Hall's principal feature is its welcoming canopy. From its illuminated underside, rainwater – which has been collected on the roof – streams downward in a programmatically controlled fashion from 184 small outlets. Like a town clock, this composition creates a time or climate clock beneath the canopy, with every droplet contributing upon impact to a gentle sonic backdrop. Upon the water's tranquil surface appears a play of expanding circular wavelets or "pitterpatterns". At night, the canopy's illuminated ceiling converts the water droplets into tiny bodies of light.

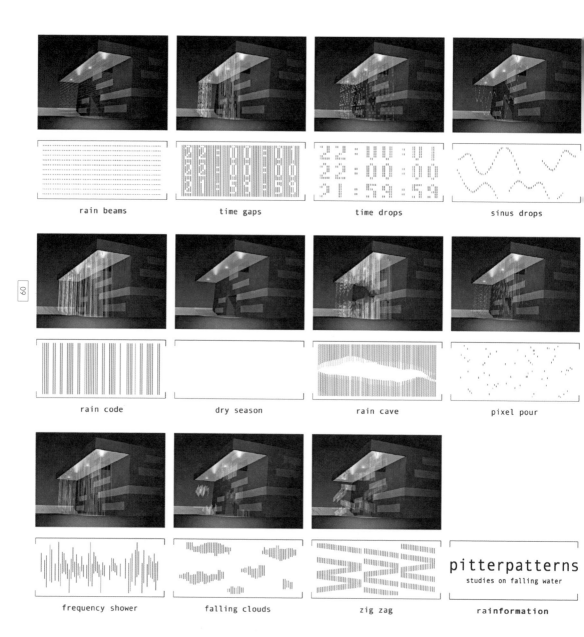

rain beams   time gaps   time drops   sinus drops

rain code   dry season   rain cave   pixel pour

frequency shower   falling clouds   zig zag

pitterpatterns
studies on falling water

rainformation

FOUNDATION / GROUND WATER Because the land under development consists of silt and clay of various consistencies, a relatively high sensitivity to settling required special attention during foundation work. The basement level takes the form of a waterproof tank of concrete, made resistant to up-welling moisture and set on monolithic bored piles that are fixed to the ground slab. The construction base rests at the northwest corner, 2.5m below the measured water table. To insure adequate groundwater diversion, a base filter layer and ring drainage were planned as safety drainage at the level of the base of the foundation. Contact between surface and ground water is prevented by a watertight layer.

STRUCTURE Load-bearing structures were executed in reinforced concrete, and partly in exposed concrete. Essentially, a construction grid of 7.5m x 5.4m was employed. Individual reinforced concrete cores and the outer walls bear loads; otherwise all levels are free of supports right up to the façades. The steel construction of the projecting canopy/ roof was attached to the concrete structure.

FAÇADE The general effect of the canted cube of the building's volume is one of a deliberately planned feeling of perceptual unease. One the one hand, the impression of massive bulk is mainly a function of its externally closed geometry, intensified by the detailing, with its sharply angular and jointless corner articulations, non-profiled material termini and flush-mounted transitions between materials. On the other hand, the division of the building's overall mass into horizontally-running anodized bands, ranging in colour from silver to brown, counteracts the massiveness of the overall volume. The anodized tones of the façades grow darker as the building rises, apparently contradicting the placement of physical weight.

© David Franck

Construction of the strip windows as double-layered "climate windows" (a window system allowing climate control without mechanical means) achieves a marked improvement in protection from summer heat, rendering additional air conditioning facilities unnecessary for the offices. With higher summer temperatures, the climate windows allow the nocturnal flushing-out of the offices, since the inner windows – sheltered from the elements and safeguarded from intruders by the outer façade – can be left open overnight, allowing cool air to stream in. Once the night air has cooled the massive, substantially exposed main building, it is ready to absorb heat again during the daytime. In sum, the climate windows offer the following advantages:

– increased comfort in wintertime via higher surface temperatures on inner panes
– a roughly 10% reduction in heating requirements
– enhancement of sound insulation toward the exterior
– protection from weathering for the sunshades in the interspaces of the climate windows

The underside of the roof/canopy and the roofed terrace were constructed as luminous ceilings of polycarbonate panelling.

ROOF / TERRACES The roof was realized as a level roof garden with an insulating sheet membrane. A central roof zone was set up as a terrace, paved with concrete blocks and delimited by a steel railing. The roof terrace is accessible from the 2nd and 3rd upper stories via two steel staircases. All horizontal cap elements for attic termini consist of anodized aluminium panelling that prolongs the façade.

© David Franck

INTERIOR WALLS Following the articulation of the building's internal structure, interior walls were executed partly as massive cores – to some degree in exposed concrete – and partly as plasterboard stud partitions. In the basement level, ancillary rooms were also partly executed in plastered masonry. In terms of colour, the various wall materials were treated differently. Aluminium baseboards, lying flush with the walls, were used.

CEILINGS   In keeping with the climate-control concept, 60% of the ceilings in offices lying toward the exterior will be left as exposed concrete. For reasons of acoustic performance, remaining surfaces in these rooms were outfitted with sound-absorptive, perforated plaster panel ceilings. All publicly accessible areas, such as hallways, waiting areas, the department of citizen's services, the district library, the municipal gallery, and parts of the 3rd upper story, were given continuous luminous ceilings of polycarbonate elements. Ceilings and walls in the more imposing multi-purpose civic hall were outfitted with sound-absorptive strip-shaped wooden elements.

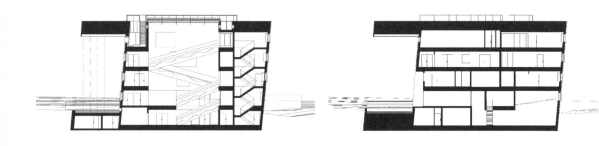

Level 1

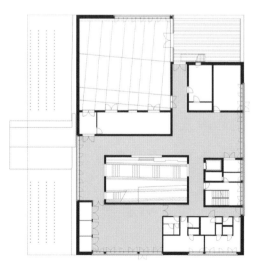

Level 2

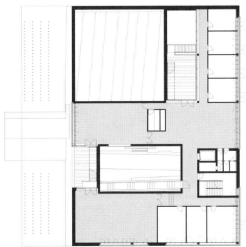

Level 3

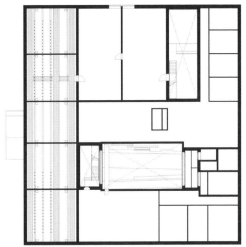

Level 4

FLOORING All access areas were given rubber nap flooring, in each case in keeping with the colour of individual stories, as visible on the façade. Offices, conference and group rooms and service areas were carpeted with a data protection pattern developed especially for the Town Hall, one also visible on the ventilation grills of the façade. Special rooms such as the events hall, the chamber for marriage ceremonies and the exercise room were given oak fillet parquet flooring.

TECHNICAL FACILITIES The climate-control concept, incorporating climate windows, makes it possible to dispense altogether with a mechanical air conditioning system. Intake and exhaust ventilation facilities are planned only for areas lying deep within the structure, and for larger spaces (the functions hall, exercise room and conference chamber). Heating facilities are provided via connection to an external heating supply.

Carpet with data-protection pattern. © David Franck

WIND.LICHT The market square, site of the WIND.LICHT, connects the actual and virtual public spaces of the town of Ostfildern. A light sculpture animated by the wind, its movements are observable on the market square itself, but also as a video projection appearing inside the Town Hall, as well as on the web pages of the town of Ostfildern.

The market square at Scharnhauser Park serves as the forecourt of the Town Hall; it is the setting of a weekly market, as well of minor celebrations. Lying between the market square and the adjoining street zone, the WIND.LICHT functions like an optical filter between the flowing street traffic and the square itself.

The WIND.LICHT consists of 16 masts each 14m high, which are inclined – like the Town Hall itself – at a 5° angle. From each mast hangs a 10m-long luminous glass-fiber cable, at whose terminus is attached a lens that projects a point of light onto the ground. In the absence of wind, the cables hang motionlessly from their masts; when the wind blows, they swing to create a dynamic network of mobile points of light that wander across the pavement. A webcam is built into each mast of the WIND.LICHT at a height of 2m, aimed at the resting positions of the points of light visible on the pavement. Images collected from all 16 masts are assembled onto a single projection screen, in a manner comparable to presentations by video surveillance systems. When the wind dies down, a regular grid of lights is displayed; when it blows, we see a mobile grid configuration, animated by natural forces.

With its integration of real and virtual public spaces, the WIND.LICHT supports an idea pursued by the town of Ostfildern, namely to play a pioneering role vis-à-vis the integration of newer media in the context of publicly funded service provisions.

Simulation of webcam images on Ostfildern's website

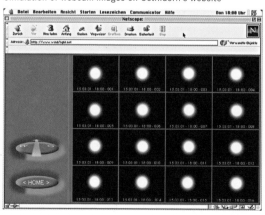

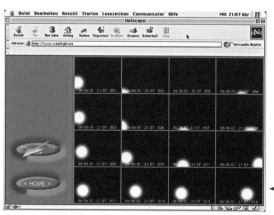

No wind   With wind

10 m

14 m

5°

Webcam

Luminous
glass-fiber cable

Mitte, Berlin

→ VERB

Stylepark (www.stylepark.com) is a website offering a database for architects, clients and design enthusiasts where more than 7,400 products from around 130 manufacturers and 840 designers are catalogued. The integration of intelligent technology and new materials in architecture is the subject of the Stylepark Case Study. How can each person's individual requirements regarding personal surroundings and comfort be addressed through the use of new technologies? How can the interaction between users and environments be changed to open up new perspectives for living in the 21st century? To answer these questions, Jürgen Mayer H. is transforming a roof apartment in Berlin into a simulation field for interactive room atmospheres, where the innovative potential of new products from manufacturers represented at Stylepark can be tested and integrated.

A case study project with Stylepark: Corridor > Jürgen Mayer H.

Corridor can be found above the skyline in Berlin. Its elongated, twisting room extends through the whole flat and connects external and internal space – the vista over the city with the vertical view to the skies. The corridor is nevertheless much more than a transit area connecting the individual living spaces with one another, separating spaces in order to create privacy. The corridor is in itself the main room of the flat. Freed of any extraneous formalities, as a space which has been created out of itself, this "extract" is able to provide the means by which unconventional, abstract spatial characteristics and liberating spatial experiences can be simulated. The connecting rooms, by contrast, take on the role of places of repose for personal renewal and privacy. In looking at the historical development of the apartment type, one can see, in the introduction of the "corridor" element, a strategy of both separating adjoining spaces as well as communication between disparate spaces. With the use of new technologies such as Global Positioning Systems, mobile phones and PDA's, communication itself becomes less dependent on spatial proximity. Doors no longer function as the primary source of control for the contact process. Removing oneself from the communication process means putting down the PDA, switching off the phone or deactivating the transmitter. In this way, the corridor itself loses its only real meaning as a separator or connecting element in the home.

Corridor is the prototype of a space that is determined neither by its spatial nor functional aspects. By utilizing the potential of technology and infrastructure it is able to create instead a "room of possibilities". Contextually, this means that the corridor reacts to the ever-changing and unpredictable moods of the dweller by being equipped with the ability to adapt: the architecture itself is fitted with the electronics of a "comfort system", offering sliding "smart walls" equipped with sound, video and projection technology, as well as specially developed reflecting colors enabling the highest quality of illuminated projections onto walls. This allows the rooms themselves to become active, moving image surfaces. The discrete yet constantly varying zones are defined through light and sound; as sounds/clouds and light/noise pulsate through the corridor, functional areas transform themselves into zones. Consisting of points of light arranged as a grid, the light/noise follows the flow of the space, and through the use of individually controlled points of light can show a wide range of graphics and texts such as info/weather, displaying the latest weather report. A linking with the sound system creates constellations such as black/holes, light/nings, search/lights and light/codings. By connecting this system to movement sensors, the user can activate a zone of light wherever he or she is situated at that particular moment.

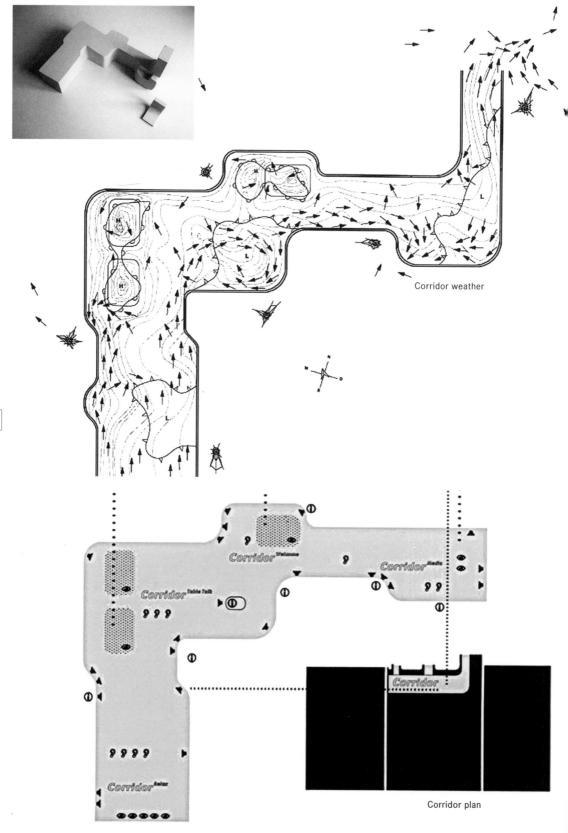

Corridor weather

Corridor plan

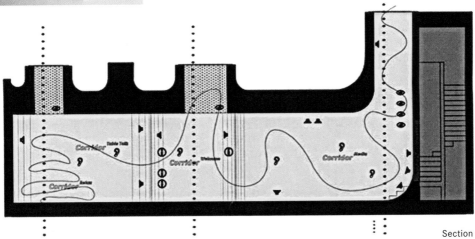

Section

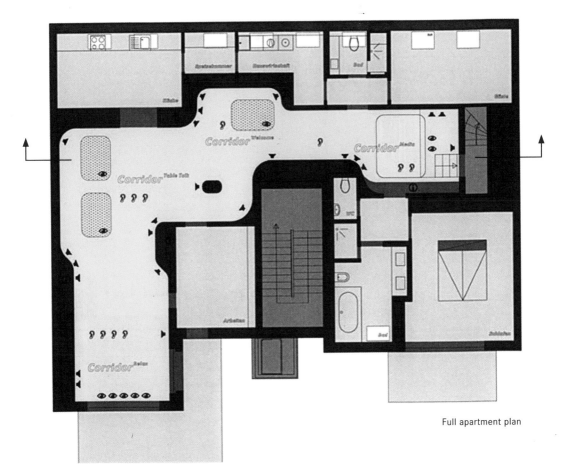

Full apartment plan

In addition, the walls and ceiling of the corridor are transformed into a scene of graphic after-images by the application of illuminated colors, slowly receding as it becomes darker. Textile surfaces on furniture, curtains, tablecloths and, in part, clothes, can also be treated as luminous material – with the effect of turning the occupant into a silhouette, still recognizable as a shadowy form against an illuminated background surface. A technical system, developed as emergency guidance lighting during power-failures, has thus been developed further and reapplied: the illuminated color becomes a temporal-spatial co-ordinate replacing the real space with a temporary light/image.

Corridor transforms living spaces into a simulation area for interactive spatial atmospheres. It is within this context that the innovative and integrative potential of manufacturers' new products, represented at Stylepark, can be put to the test. A new area of dialogue between the natural and technologically created, spatially dynamic scenarios has thus been created – a test lab for new ways of living.

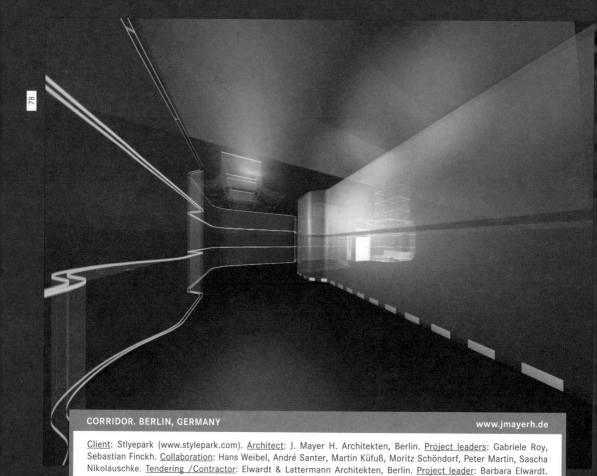

CORRIDOR. BERLIN, GERMANY www.jmayerh.de

Client: Stlyepark (www.stylepark.com). Architect: J. Mayer H. Architekten, Berlin. Project leaders: Gabriele Roy, Sebastian Finckh. Collaboration: Hans Weibel, André Santer, Martin Küfuß, Moritz Schöndorf, Peter Martin, Sascha Nikolauschke. Tendering /Contractor: Elwardt & Lattermann Architekten, Berlin. Project leader: Barbara Elwardt. Light planning: Studio Dinnebier, Berlin. Project leader: Anne Boissel. Control technical equipment: GIRA. Color design: SIKKENS.

Plywood seating unit

OMA, Rotterdam

Prada sponge
stereolithographed panels

Gel mat seating cushions

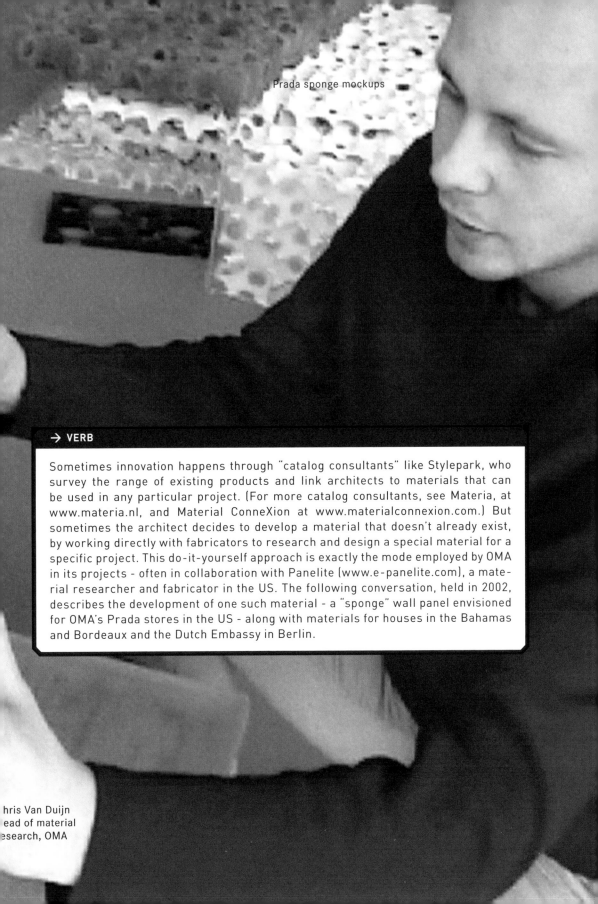

Prada sponge mockups

hris Van Duijn
ead of material
esearch, OMA

→ VERB

Sometimes innovation happens through "catalog consultants" like Stylepark, who survey the range of existing products and link architects to materials that can be used in any particular project. (For more catalog consultants, see Materia, at www.materia.nl, and Material ConneXion at www.materialconnexion.com.) But sometimes the architect decides to develop a material that doesn't already exist, by working directly with fabricators to research and design a special material for a specific project. This do-it-yourself approach is exactly the mode employed by OMA in its projects - often in collaboration with Panelite (www.e-panelite.com), a material researcher and fabricator in the US. The following conversation, held in 2002, describes the development of one such material - a "sponge" wall panel envisioned for OMA's Prada stores in the US - along with materials for houses in the Bahamas and Bordeaux and the Dutch Embassy in Berlin.

I've been involved in this research on materials since we started to work on the Prada projects in early 2000. The starting point of the whole process was a desire to find non-systematic ways to hang and display clothes in the New York and Los Angeles stores, without hierarchy and without hangbars anywhere on the walls. In the study models we came up with the idea of using a sponge, whose perforations offered this possibility of non-systematic forms of display. We tested this idea with different backlights and sponges of different colors. This was not a specific project decision yet, but when Rem saw it we decided to consider it as the actual wall material by simply blowing up the sponge from the 1:100 model to 1:1 scale. We studied its geometry regarding the size and position of the perforations by arranging balloons filled with water in an open box, casting plaster or concrete around them, and then taking the balloons out. We also tried it with basketballs, but we found that it was much easier with balloons.

In the meantime we also contacted sponge manufacturers to find out why these foams didn't exist with bigger perforations. It seems that chemically it is not possible to make them bigger, but there is also a very obvious explanation – as the material is expanded it loses density and eventually consistency to the point of collapse. So we realized that we would have to make them mechanically.

We worked with the industrial designer Vincent de Rijk, who has been in-volved in OMA's projects since the mid-eighties, mostly in the production of resin models. He is the in-house plastics expert. In his workshop we built models with different polyurethanes, soft rubbers and silicone.
Soft materials deteriorated over time, and we also realized that the mate-rial used in these walls had to be flame-retardant to comply with fire regu-lations. This seemed to imply the use of aluminum or concrete instead of plastic, but one important aspect that we always wanted to achieve was the translucency of the material. If you hold these plastic models against the light you get different rays and transparencies which give depth to the ma-terial, making it look soft and tactile.
We decided then to ask BGB Enterprises, a plastics company based in LA, to look into the possibilities of obtaining the appropriate flame-retardance in a translucent polyester, since the only existing plastics that were flame-retardant – produced by BASF – were opaque and dark. We also decided to work with Panelite, another company based in LA that develops new materials, in order to help us in our research on finishes, since as an American company they know a lot about the specific codes

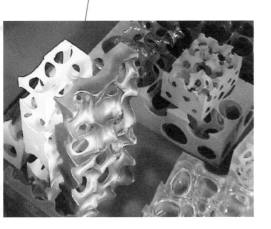

that we had to comply with. Panelite's collaboration was also needed to find a way to produce these polyester panels in large quantities. Defining the perforations with balloons allowed us to produce a master sample, a sponge prototype with the geometry and scale of the openings that we wanted to match, but it obviously wasn't effective for large-scale production. Our first model-shop mold was produced by splitting the prototype in two halves, into half-bubbles, and then casting silicone around it. This allowed us to produce 60 of these panels, which were then placed against each other and behind each other to check if the geometry produced by their combination worked. The system itself did work, but the discontinuity between holes that was produced from one panel to the next was very disturbing. The half-holes at the edges had to line up, which made the situation much more complicated, since you have two geometries to worry about. With Panelite we decided to make a 3D model of the sponge from which they could mill out an aluminum mold for casting the panels in resin, which

sounds very simple. This has the advantage that we could create the sponge exactly in the geometry that we wanted, with the perfect sharpness, perfect openings, etc., and also make it work as a mold that would release very easily. We went through a phase of approximately half a year during which we studied the sponges and their regularities – because although it

doesn't look like it, in fact the structure is very regular. We decided that we could make the panels 3 meters high and 1.5 meters wide in one mold if we wanted to, and we started to play with these computer models, making renderings, making computer diagrams.

The first intermediate step before milling the molds was stereolithography, which we used to cut two identical panels that form a continuous geometry of the holes when placed one behind the other. The only problem with identical panels is that you can see right through the geometry – you can tell that the two panels are actually the same, and this wouldn't look good in the store. So we went back to the computer model in order to make two different panels – a front and a back one – and two molds. We manipulated and modified the geometry, made aluminum molds with a CNC milling machine, did a lot of strength and durability tests on different plastics, and developed a system of nipples in the sponge molds that would allow for the two parts of the mold to form a water-tight seal but also to be taken apart easily. So actually the key detail in this whole mold is the hole, the thing that you don't see, and developing the geometry of this strange nipple is what took us the most time.

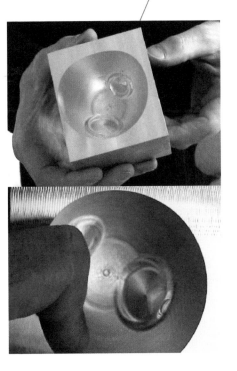

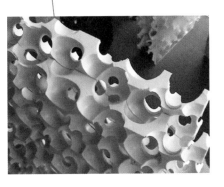

All these little things were revealed in this process. We also found out that milling the aluminum molds took a lot longer than we thought – six weeks instead of the expected four days, with the machine running twenty-four hours a day. So it's an enormous and very expensive process to make a mold this size, and the actual mold has to be eight times this size – four times its height and two times its width.

→ VERB

In the end, the Prada sponge is being produced in Italy (with a different manufacter and with slightly more traditional techniques than the ones described here, Chris says). It is being applied in the Prada Los Angeles store, open as of summer 2004.

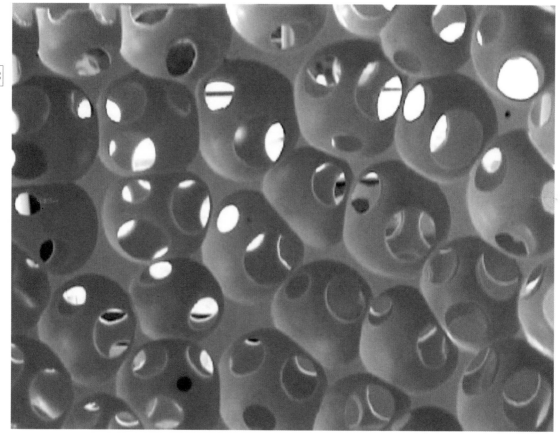

One side-product of the sponge is a bubble mat made of rubber. Our first idea was to use it in the dressing rooms, where people stand barefoot, and for the NY store we thought of using it in the lower level, where you would come down from the wave onto a big mat of 8 by 10 meters. We tested this mat in gel, silicone, and in normal, transparent polyurethane rubbers, and now we are testing the seams and checking the possibilities for having continuous geometries from one mat to the other. When you try to use this type of unconventional material for the whole space you run into problems like finding the right way to glue the seams together and make sure that it will last, and also to find someone who will install these mats, because there is no guarantee, no experience. So even though the geometry doesn't change, getting to the final product takes a lot more than the geometry alone.

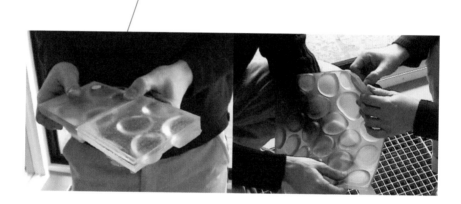

We also wanted to use big mats of rubber as seating elements, based on a seat used in OMA's project for the Second Stage Theater in New York. That seat was made of a gel used in bicycle saddles, which is of course very ergonomic, but which is usually covered in a fabric. In the medical sector it's also used in hospital beds. We wanted them 3cm thick and as big as possible, much bigger than the sizes available from the manufacturer. The coating they used broke at the edges, and ended up being replaced by new coatings which don't age like the previous ones. It's not a product or material we invented, but just tried to change the size and shape in which it was produced.

Finally we would like the soft and transparent qualities of these materials to also apply to the hangers themselves, which will be made out of rubber that should be bendable or squeezable but nevertheless resistant enough for heavy coats. Hopefully Prada will pick up this idea for the shops instead of

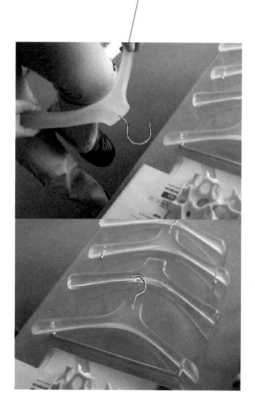

the wooden hangers used now or the normal plastic hangers in the market, which are injection-molded, 2mm thick and hollow inside.

In this plastic research you have to choose between very industrial products with high investment costs, or you can have something like a prototype, hand-cast and with this tactile feeling. For this specific hanger we would like to combine both – to use industrial techniques to produce a very simple result: a solid plastic soft rubber hanger. But somehow to make it is not as simple as it looks.

We have also collaborated with Panelite in the design of a bathroom for a house in the Bahamas, in which we wanted to make monolithic objects with curved, organic forms. In this project the structure of the building will be a black steel shell assembled on site, but most of the components will be produced overseas, in Europe or in the US, shipped there, and inserted into the structure. Panelite produces a flexible honeycomb panel that we wanted to use, but the problem you always run into with plastics is that you either have a very industrial material, like polycarbonates or acrylics, which you need huge facilities for and can't modify beyond what the company already produces with the molds they have, or you have workshop plastics like polyester and rubbers which you can make yourself. What we would like to do in

the Bahamas project is a panel that combines the two types of plastic – o
the one hand it has this very industrial product, the PET plastic, that we
then combine with a layer of hard rubber with glass fiber in it. Because of
the combination of the two, we can use the plastic as a mold, shape it, an
then brush on the rubber with glass fiber to keep it in position. So we don'
need very expensive molds to make three-dimensional shapes, but we jus†
bend the wavecore material in a very simple wooden frame, add the rubbe
on, and it stays like that. In this way we try to combine the benefits of bot
the industrial product and the hand-made product, which is not as perfect
or regular as an acrylic surface, but which is much more tactile.
We have also been doing a lot of research with aluminum, starting with the
floor of the house in Bordeaux. This is an aluminum sample produced almost as one would make a cake – you mix aluminum powder with silicone
and other materials that react under pressure, you put it in the oven, and i
starts to rise. Then it is closed off on the sides with layers of aluminum.
Given its extreme lightness and strength, this material is now being tested
for applications in the car industry, especially for the production of chassis

or frames as an alternative to the big steel tube structures. We also thought that it could be blown up as a solution to the Prada sponge, but as with the sponge material, the bigger it gets the thinner the material and the less coherent it becomes.

In the Dutch embassy building in Berlin we are using a double-glazing system that we initiated, though it was not developed by us, made of thin glass tubes inserted between the two exterior glass sheets. With this system the façades are not transparent, but you can still see through the panel. The glass tubes are extremely fragile, but as a composed structure it is very resistant and insulates very well. In a parallel test, we have looked for ways to obtain translucent steel – basically using a honeycomb structure clad in polyester. It's completely water-tight, and it would be a way to make insulating, load-bearing translucent walls.

SCI-Arc, Los Angeles, 2003

92

(e)^3 _ **emergence . effect . environment** > Marta Malé-Alemany

Marta Malé-Alemany and José Pedro Sousa > Today the digital revolution has reached its first stage of maturity. After new technologies introduced greater versatility in tradition-al design processes, recent research has focused on applying the potentials of the digital to generate and fabricate architectural forms.

The integration of Computer Aided Manufacturing (CAM) processes into architecture began at the end of the 20th century. Widely used in several industrial fields (automotive, aero-space, etc.), digital fabrication systems are being appropriated by architects to develop building technologies in new directions. As CAD/CAM technology becomes less expensive, different tendencies distinguish its architectural application: larger offices (Gehry, Foster, Grimshaw) have used it to execute complex geometries and optimize building components, while smaller practices (Bernhard Franken, dECOi, William Massie, ShoP) are incorporating it into their design agenda. While the computer has been the medium for developing and communicating architectural designs, numerically driven (CNC) machines promote their translation into the physical world by fabricating non-standard forms with extreme preci-sion. By superseding the limitations imposed by industrial standardization, CAM offers a shift from mass-production to 'mass-customization' modes, challenging the conditions for developing architectural projects.

(e)^3 fits within this last trend, concerned with exploring the conceptual and material oppor-tunities that emerge from these processes. Supported by associative parametric software, the project embraces a non-linear condition: if proportion and scale are variable param-eters, then the design is able to respond at any given time to the interference of changing material, manufacturing, or assembly changing constraints.

(e)^3 is an architectural construction that explores the concept of emergence: from design and fabrication to physical experience. Described in three terms – emergence, effect, environment – the project engages space to materialize the aesthetics of a variable field, producing emergent perceptive effects. Installed at the SCI-Arc Architecture Gallery in the summer of 2003, the project used a digital design process to produce parametrically-described versions of a 'hypothetical' project, making it possible to examine the design in different configurations and thus create a specific solution for the gallery. The project was then fabricated using CNC technologies to produce non-standard shapes with complex geometries, providing an efficiency to solve time and budget constraints. CAD/CAM proce-dures, materials, and fabrication processes were used to build a project entirely conceived and developed with the computer.

(e)³ is a freestanding wall construction, an 18.3m long by x 2.4m high steel structure that supports a set of 46 curved translucent panels. It stands aligned with the gallery entrance, parallel to a perimeter wall displaying a 1:1 scale elevation drawing of the digital data that generated the design. The 1.8m space between defines a corridor that invites entering in the middle of the installation, while the structure allows one to wander through and pass underneath. Under changing lightning conditions, numerous visual effects define the spatial experience: shadows merge with reflections of glowing acrylic surfaces, distorted body silhouettes appear behind the faceted curvature of translucent panels, and sections of the elevation drawing are framed by openings in the wall, creating an emergent visual mosaic with different levels of resolution.

DESIGN PROCESS To develop (e)³, an interactive digital model was created using associative parametric software to generate a project that "emerges" from data constructions, interconnecting local (component) and global (whole assembly) parameters.
The design began with a parametric mosaic, a rectangular serial pattern that repeats with a progressive rhythm. This field is then extended, with proportional outlines arrayed in hidden symmetries and rotations. It offers a system of repetitive parts arranged in non-repetitive ways, providing a solution for mass-producing identical components without compromising the aesthetics of a more variable organization.
Like a dynamic typology, the field can be adjusted by parameters to fit specific architectural conditions and dictate the final dimensions of the panels and structure. By grouping identical elements in families by size, the panelization system resolves several questions: how to formally differentiate components, create surface effects, and optimize fabrication. The differentiation of components is based on coupling the idea of *scale* with that of *resolution*, to produce the digital aesthetic of a large, pixelated surface. Parametric modeling helped in mapping (local) relationships of proximity between panels, to generate a gray-

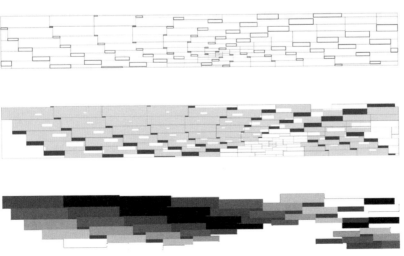

Pixelated surface

scale (global) image representation or index of the whole assembly. This 'map' was converted into a three-dimensional surface, reproduced like a fractal in different resolutions. While smaller (low-resolution) panels become almost flat, larger (high-resolution) ones turn into highly faceted (pixelated) versions of the same shape, now bigger and more three-dimensional. As a result, these differential curvatures create an array of surface effects that change from one location to another. A more subtle effect emerges when looking across the faceted individual surfaces; although the panels are not aligned, the smaller grain – the matching 'pixels' from one panel to the next – turns the installation into a fragmented yet continuous whole. Grouping families also offers a fundamental advantage in developing a certain economy of fabrication, which translates, for instance, into pulling multiple copies off a single mold in the process of vacuum forming.

With this underlying systematicity (e)^3 lies between mass-production and mass-customization, with repetitive fabrication processes like vacuum-forming contrasted with the CNC milling of distinctive faceted surfaces.

FABRICATION (e)^3 was fabricated and installed in 3 weeks using the 3-axis CNC mill at SCI-Arc, subcontracted local workshops for welding the structure and vacuum-forming the plastic, and student help for overall assembly.

The manufacturing of panels required CNC milled foam molds as forms for vacuum-molding. In the search for a material that would be structural, easily formable, and offer the desired translucency, several plastics were tested: acrylic, styrene, polyethylene, ABS and others.

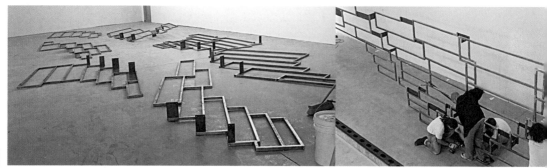

Given transportation and storage constraints, the structure was built in parts, allowing easy re-assembly for another venue. The sections (maximum 4.9m x 2.4m) were connected in series to create a single, large-scale steel structure.

The 18.3m x 2.4m elevation drawing was contour-cut with a plotter on white vinyl, applied to the existing wall (previously painted in green) in sections based on the plotter width.

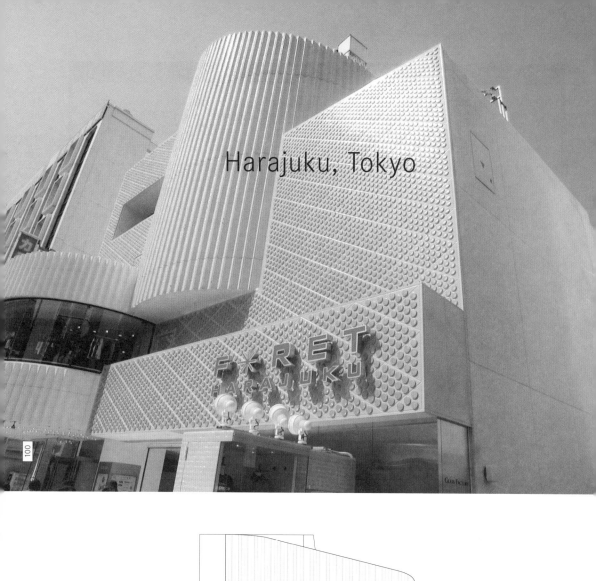

Harajuku, Tokyo

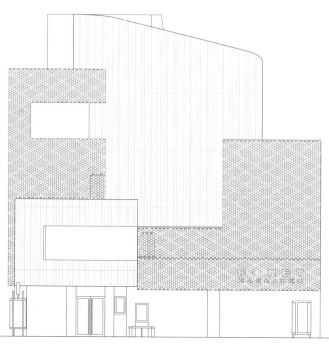

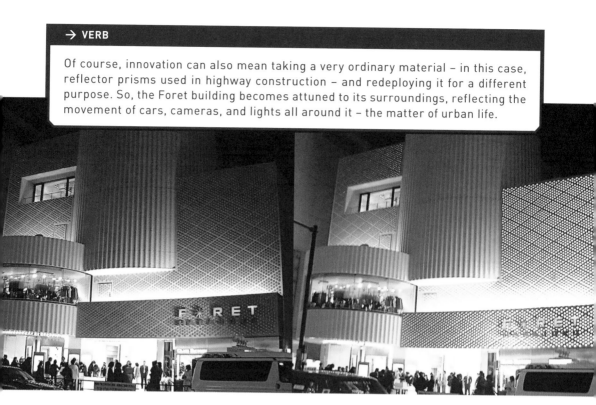

Foret > Klein Dytham Architecture

CAT EYES Foret is the sister fashion store of Laforet, which KDa renewed in spring 2001 and is located some 100m away along the same street.

To create a new image for the façade and entrance area befitting this young and trendy area, KDa affixed 6271 white round 'delineator' road reflectors onto a bright green façade. The reflectors generate attention by reformatting and reflecting the activity of the city back to the passerby. During the day the façade sparkles in the sun light, and seen obliquely a rainbow of light shimmers across the façade.

At night the façade pulsates, reflecting the light of the surrounding shops, neon signs and car headlights. The 'delineator' reflector prisms reflect the light back to its source no matter what angle it enters the lens at. The light from a camera flash lights up the whole façade, each reflector lighting up and sending the light straight back to the camera. It appears as if the whole façade has been turned on and off in an instant.

The reflecting theme was taken through to the floor, where white 'glassbead' paint - normally used for traffic crossings - covers the entire entrance area.

Encased solar powered LEDs dot the floor, flashing during darkness, again attracting people's attention.

The existing showcases on either side of the main building were completely covered with rectangular reflectors too, completing the composition.

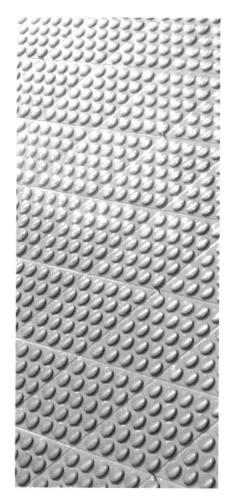

Elevation

Section

Detail of delineator

Base:
Stainless steel t=1.5
finish:
SUS bent panel t=1.5
+ stoving paint
Delineator: polycarbonate lens
+ ABS resin made colored base plate
+ aluminum frame

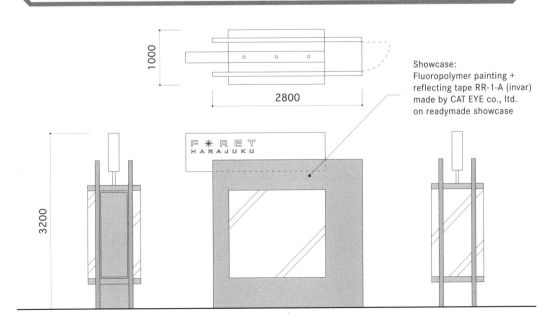

FORET HARAJUKU "CAT EYES". TOKYO, JAPAN   www.klein-dytham.com

Architects: Klein Dytham Architecture. Site: Harajuku, Tokyo. Completion: 2002. Facade design: Klein Dytham Architecture. Project team: Astrid Klein, Mark Dytham, Yukinari Hisayama. Client: Mori Bldg. Ryutsu Group. Construction: 01.2002-02 . 2002 Ishizue Co., ltd. Delineator production: Kashimura Co.,ltd.

1000

2800

Showcase:
Fluoropolymer painting +
reflecting tape RR-1-A (invar)
made by CAT EYE co., ltd.
on readymade showcase

3200

F✱RET
HARAJUKU

Beacon Offices > Klein Dytham Architecture

Beacon is a new advertising agency formed by the merger of 3 separate agencies: Leo Burnet, D'Arcy and Dentsu. The newly formed company wanted to move into offices that would reflect their new approach to advertising and allow for a new working style, with communication among the agency's staff of 300 seen as key. The new office was intended to generate crossover between the staff at every possible opportunity. More talking, more chance meetings, more 'what are you doing', more 'what's that you're working on'.

Many of the initial meetings with Beacon took place at Deluxe, our shared open studio. Lots of meetings happen at the same time in Deluxe, with no real division. Everybody always knows what's going on, and the chance for exchange between the 5 companies that share the space is very strong. Beacon wanted something similar, something as flexible – an office that could regroup as new brands emerged and old brands disappeared. This meant turning away from the enclosed offices and cubicles that everyone was used to and moving to very open offices.

The JR Tokyu Meguro building is built over the Yamanote train line and the new Mekama line station, which gives the building a column-free space 60m long by 15m wide. The long side of the plan faces west, with stunning views; the core wall faces east, with the south and north windows looking up and down the train tracks. This suggested leaving the west side of the building free for all the open-plan desks, so everyone could enjoy the daylight and the views. Correspondingly, the meeting and multipurpose areas were positioned in a long line adjacent to the core wall. This accentuated the length of the building, making the overall space more dynamic and following the energy of the tracks below the building.

11F Women floor. Capsule space

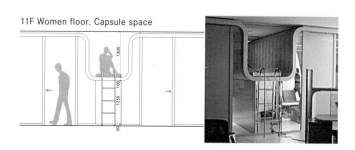

12F Community floor. Chat space

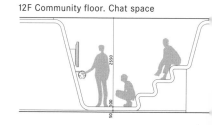

To accommodate the need for some of the meeting and multipurpose areas to be enclosed and others to be open, we developed a ribbon that connects the different rooms – acting as a ceiling in some rooms, a wall or a stage area in others. Sometimes the ribbon is glazed, sometimes it is left open to allow the space to spill out into the main office. There are no enclosed private offices, even for the directors. Everyone has their own private workstation, but sits only a few steps from the ribbon where one can find a small space to have a private conversation or a quiet meeting. The 6 directors do not even have their own desks – they work around a 12m long dining table, together with the company president. The idea is to break down the formality of the management area: anyone within the company can pull up one of the 20 dining chairs around the table and chat with the directors.

Beacon decided upon four floor themes to divide the agency: Woman, Man, Family and Community. On the Woman's floor, a hair salon and beauty center form a part of the ribbon, spilling out from an open 'stage' area of the space. The Family floor revolves around a fully functional kitchen with cooking and laundry facilities. New washing products can be tested and demonstrated here. Materials and colors, too, revolve around the themed floors – the ribbon on the Man's floor is steel, the ribbon on the Family floor is wood, and the ribbon on the Woman's floor is pink snake skin!

Of course the office has the dual purpose of acting as a showroom for future clients, as advertising for the agency itself. But beyond this, the office is seen almost as a living room – after all, you spend more of your awake time in the office than you do at home. In fact, Beacon sees the move as 'okaerinasai' – a welcome home – since they too have gone back 'home', to the downtown in Meguro where they are closer to consumers than their previous bases in the business districts of Tokyo. So, too, the office offers a warm, welcoming place to work.

14F Family floor. Kitchen

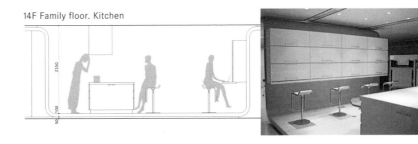

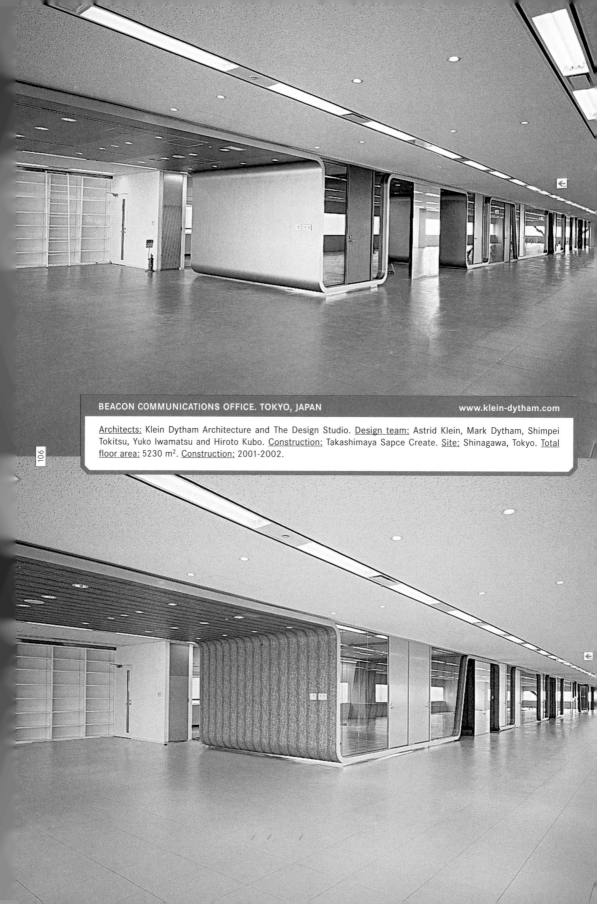

BEACON COMMUNICATIONS OFFICE. TOKYO, JAPAN

www.klein-dytham.com

Architects: Klein Dytham Architecture and The Design Studio. Design team: Astrid Klein, Mark Dytham, Shimpei Tokitsu, Yuko Iwamatsu and Hiroto Kubo. Construction: Takashimaya Sapce Create. Site: Shinagawa, Tokyo. Total floor area: 5230 m². Construction: 2001-2002.

Matter is not just the material of which a building is made, but also the materials of the construction process: the means by which the building is built, as much as the final constitution of the building itself. Takuya Onishi has been studying the use of the lightest possible material – air – to rebuild structures damaged by earthquakes in disaster areas, by means of an inflatable bubble stabilizer. The buildings are ordinary, but the matter of their (re)construction is not.

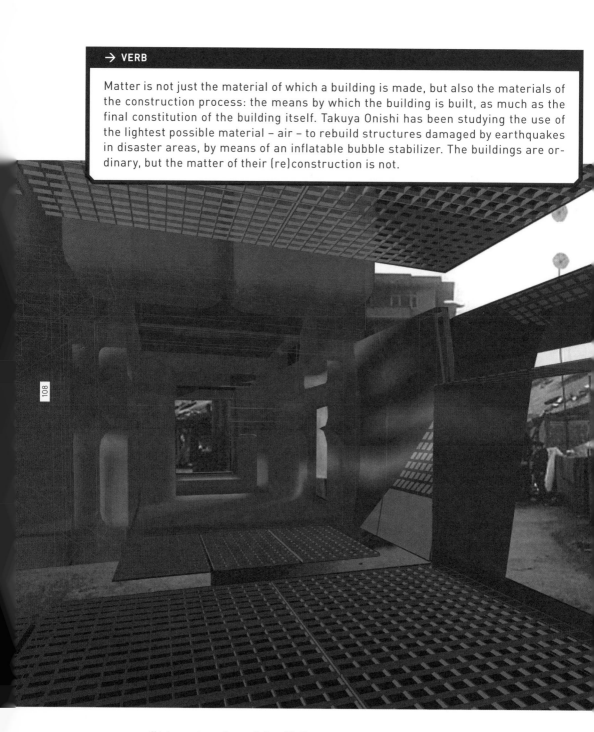

"Hundreds of buildings have collapsed, but there is no one here who can help."
The Independent, 13th November 1999

nflatable Bubble Stabilizer > Launchpad 05 Takuya Onishi
)esign for the reconstruction of the city with airbags after an earthquake
Research conducted at the Architectural Association, London

1. SITUATION - DUZCE, TURKEY 19TH NOVEMBER 1999 Disaster came again in the early evening. 7.2 on the Richter scale. Hitting the edge of the same region as the devastating trem-
or of the 17th August, which measured 7.4. The tremor was quickly followed by at least five
aftershocks.
Eighteen days after the disaster I visited Duzce, the seismic center of the second earthquake. Duzce is a small city approximately four hours drive from Istanbul.
Approximately 12% of the buildings there were totally collapsed; 25% had minor damage
and remained empty. Their former inhabitants made tents in front of them.
Observation: In post-disaster situations, buildings with minor damage are hazardous. While
damage might be slight the structures are, nevertheless, uninhabitable. Pulling down these
buildings is costly and involves huge effort. Consequently, hundreds of buildings with minor
damage remain on the earthquake site for long periods. They are empty, useless boxes. But
despite their vulnerability, these buildings are still home to the locals. In the memorable
words of a tent dweller, "We want to stay in the same place."

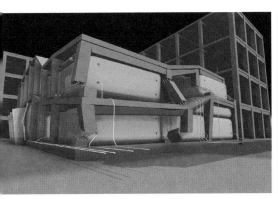 

The first priority is "getting there." This project is to find a way of stabilizing volatile build-ings so that earthquake victims can continue to inhabit them. I studied the idea of using a inflatable bubble stabilizer.

Minor-damage buildings had become critical points in this post-disaster situation. Almost all of the furniture and equipment had been removed by their owners, or by thieves. People did not have enough space for their property.

The 'minor-damage' buildings had remained on the earthquake site for a long time as use-less, empty boxes. Hundreds of people were living in tents in front of these buildings.

I thought: if buildings are totally collapsed, rescue people and remove the rubble as soon as possible. And if buildings are OK, fine, stay at home.

But what about minor-damage buildings? What do you do?

"We want to stay in the same place…"

OK. Why don't they return to the place where they used to be? Because the empty build-ings are still standing!

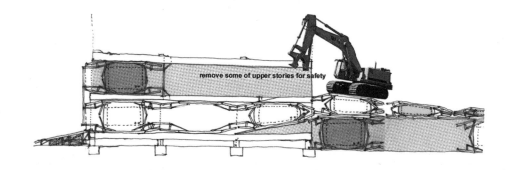

remove some of upper stories for safety

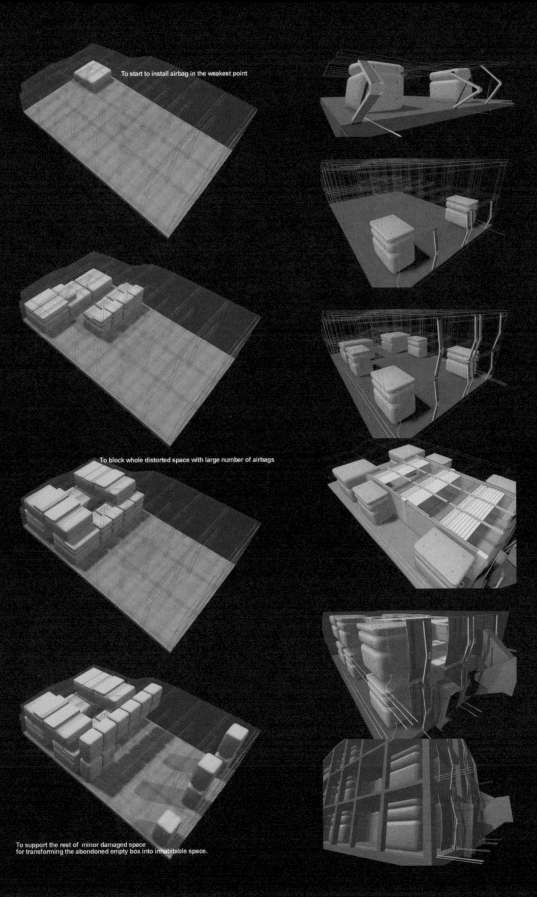

To start to install airbag in the weakest point

To block whole distorted space with large number of airbags

To support the rest of minor damaged space
for transforming the abondoned empty box into inhabitable space.

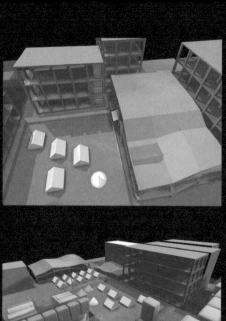

inner view: 01 (18)

2. THE PROCESS: STABILIZING MINOR-DAMAGE BULIDINGS,
ENABLING PEOPLE TO GO BACK HOME

1. Reach the site with a temporary infrastructure supported by airbags.
2. Install inflatable stabilizer into buildings with minor damage and inflate.
3. Cast concrete between the airbags and the damaged structure.
4. Remove airbags to reveal stable, hollow spaces within buildings.

3. THE SITE MODEL A small camp site at the edge of Duzce. I met friendly local kids in this small camp site, a square surrounded by various types of damaged buildings: half-distorted building types, slightly tilted building types, minor-damage building types and totally collapsed building types.
When I visited the site for the second time, there were 18 tents on the site, enough for only 72 people. Only 14% of the local population could stay on the site. Where are the other 86%?

4. MAKING A PROTOTYPE INFLATABLE STRUCTURE The prototype has to be able to be carried by container and installed easily.

Try this at home: lay a plastic garbage bag on a table. Put somebody on top, or maybe a heavy dog. A little air pressure does the trick. You will see that the person or the animal will be lifted - do it slowly, or you'll get dizzy. The only problem is that it will be difficult for the volunteer on top of the bag to keep his balance.

With more pressure, inflatable cushions can be used to lift extremely heavy bodies, even if they weigh somewhere in the region of 120 tons.

While I was exploring the making of a suitcase-size inflatable prototype, I had read reports concerning an American rescue company that was producing an airlift bag that could support 22 tons: approximately an 8m x 8m x 20cm concrete slab!

5. CONCLUSION 56% of earthquake victims can return home as a result of the stabilizer. It is hard not to be disappointed about the 44% for whom returning is still a dream. However, as an architectural student, I believe in the potency of architecture to provide a continuing strategy for resolving the earthquake problem.

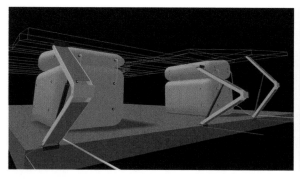 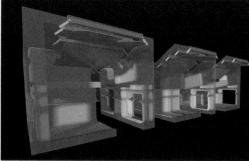

Inner-Skin House > Milligram Studio / Tomoyuki Utsumi

For the sake of easy on-site construction and to reduce loads on the loose ground of the site, the framework of this house is made of general-purpose lightweight steel members. The building, including its fixtures and fittings, is divided as far as possible into "skeleton" and "infill," and construction was also divided into these two stages.

The first stage was the skeleton construction, built within exacting legal limits, to create a highly flexible structure. The second stage was the infill operation. This process began after the owners, a couple, were already living in the house, and it was carried out with their collaboration. Our challenge here was to leave the inner plan loose enough at this point to adapt everything later to the owner's requirements.

The skeleton is seen as an open infrastructure whose transparency leaves its components exposed as far as possible. This allows the infill to be done in DIY (do-it-yourself) style, even with the owners living in the house, using the secondary connection system and reflecting the owners' private lifestyle to the greatest possible extent.

Exploring this concept, we devised a solution for an interior that can be separated from the skeleton, that is, the "membrane" or "inner-skin" system. Tensioned membranes create horizontal and vertical surfaces which do not sag under the force of gravity. Although these membranes are very light, they acquire sufficient architectural strength and can work as more than just simple partitions between rooms. Compared to traditional interior components, this "inner-skin" system is extremely lightweight, and is modularized so that various combinations with a variety of optional functional components are easily obtained.

We have seen that, through our constant improvements on this system, the owners themselves are able to plan, change and arrange their own living space quite freely – which was our real aim in this project.

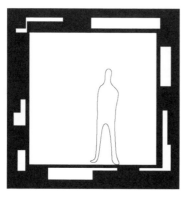

Normally the space between the interior wall and the exterior wall remains untouched and unused.

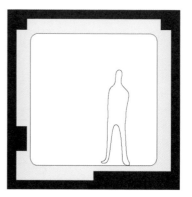

The Inner-skin house has an interior membrane wall, enabling the gap space to be used.

© Takeshi Taira

Indirect lighting - we can feel the space in-between.

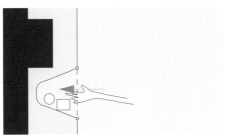

A closet - we can put things inside the space.

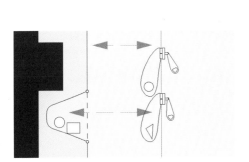

It is also possible to change the parts of the 'inner skin'.

A fastener - we can look, touch and reach into the space.

© Takeshi Taira

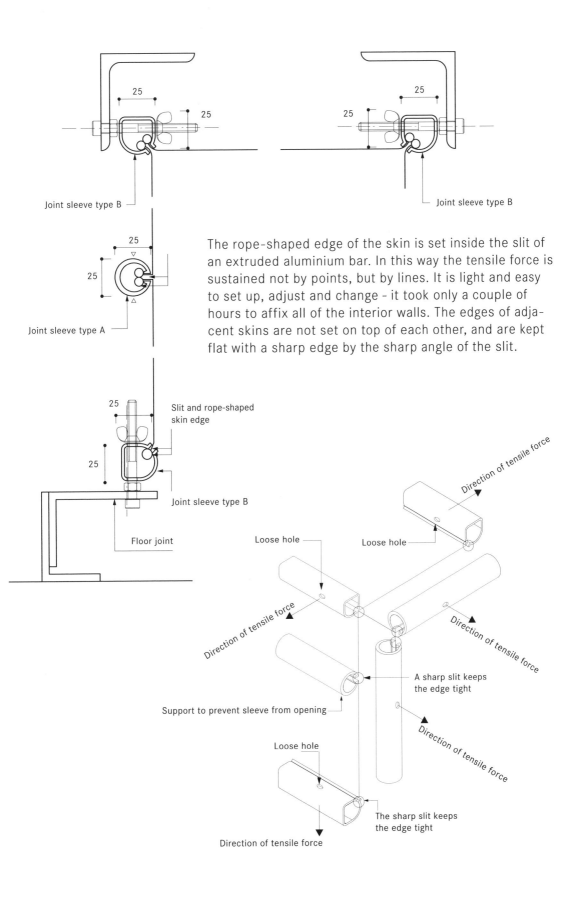

25

25

Joint sleeve type B

25

25

25

Joint sleeve type A

The rope-shaped edge of the skin is set inside the slit of an extruded aluminium bar. In this way the tensile force is sustained not by points, but by lines. It is light and easy to set up, adjust and change - it took only a couple of hours to affix all of the interior walls. The edges of adjacent skins are not set on top of each other, and are kept flat with a sharp edge by the sharp angle of the slit.

25

25

Joint sleeve type B

25

25

Slit and rope-shaped skin edge

Joint sleeve type B

Floor joint

Loose hole

Loose hole

Direction of tensile force

Direction of tensile force

Direction of tensile force

Direction of tensile force

A sharp slit keeps the edge tight

Support to prevent sleeve from opening

Loose hole

The sharp slit keeps the edge tight

Direction of tensile force

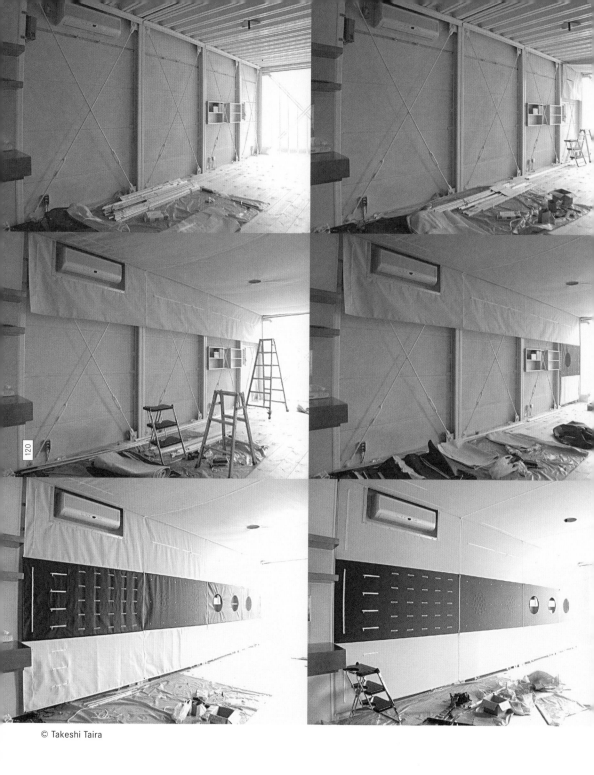

© Takeshi Taira

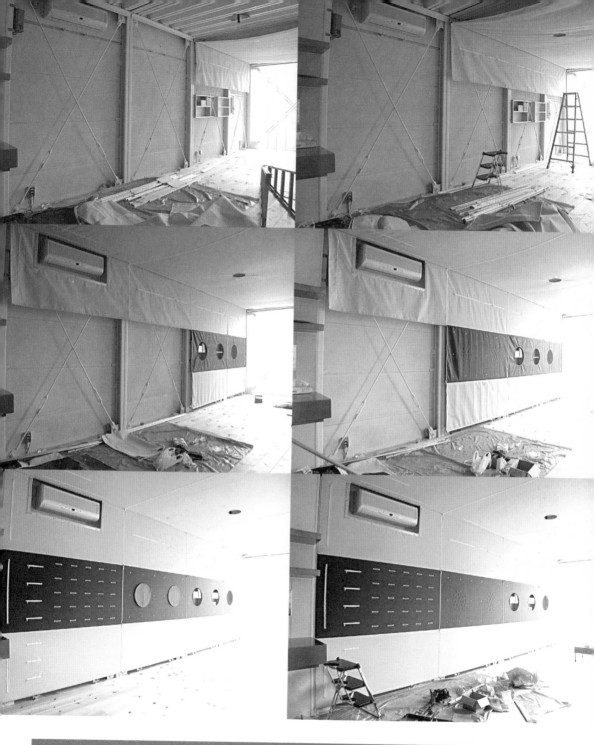

INNER-SKIN HOUSE. TOKYO, JAPAN

www.milligram.ne.jp

Skeleton: Tomoyuki Utsumi (Milligram Studio). Infill patented by: Tomoyuki Utsumi (Milligram Studio) + tai_tai studio + Taiyo Kogyo Co., Ltd.

The Moment When Materials Sublimate

Integrist Masahiro Ikeda / MIAS

Lecture at RAS gallery in Barcelona, April 2003

ARCHITECTURE = NONLINEAR INTEGRATION BETWEEN MATERIALS

The word *material* means more than just substance itself. Of course this is one aspect, but perhaps it is also accurate to consider it as a set of conditions. Instead of seeing material as the domain of engineering and the design of building elements (columns, beams, slabs), we could broaden the meaning of material to encompass the wide variety of conditions and relationships that exist within a building; in this sense, material is equivalent to the relationship between substances and conditions. Various environmental qualities could be included in this concept of material: light, air, temperature and sound may be treated as substances, and their corresponding performance requirements (such as acoustic or thermal insulation) may be treated as conditions. The definition of material as substance plus conditions can also be extended to the various people involved with a design. It is a seemingly endless list: the client, the designer, consultants, contractors, end-users... I am interested in the way a single design is generated from the combined awareness and knowledge of each person concerned.

Based on this idea of material, I wish to examine examples of how to find a single solution from the relationships between various substances and conditions by considering them all as one, examining architecture as a form of *nonlinear integration*. Explanation is impossible using only a single project, so I will proceed by showing several projects at the same time, as much as possible in chronological order, and revealing their interrelationships. All of these projects are intimately connected, and within their chronological order, the evolving set of nonlinear integrations may also be considered to comprise a single system.

Such nonlinear integrations are not unusual, but are relatively common in the world. Until now, we have only attempted to understand linear systems with simple rules, developed by processes of trial-and-error. However, if we alter relationships slightly by introducing nonlinear integrations, other things may unexpectedly emerge in a kind of chain reaction. The results are fascinating and important.

INTEGRIST

One special aspect of the Japanese education system is that upon entering architecture school, one must then decide whether to follow the path of the architect or the engineer. So at university the study of architecture and engineering occur simultaneously; having made a choice between them, one joins a specialized university laboratory, and only after graduating and finding employment does the real design activity begin.

There are currently very few people with the title of architect who are able to do the engineering for their own projects, and very few people with the title of engineer who are responsible for the design of entire buildings. I do not fit into the traditionally conceived roles of either the architect or the engineer, and am searching for a new professional role for the architect. Could there be a profession that straddles both disciplines and no longer acknowledges the boundary between them? I currently seem to have the position of *integrist*, with opportunities to become involved with architectural design.

The role of the *integrist* could be defined as one who integrates all elements beyond the domain of architecture into sublimation. This does not seem particularly new if one reflects upon the original definition of the architect, as "chief builder." Looking back on times past, the architect was involved in both design and construction; gradually, however, the architect ceased to be an engineer. I am now contemplating a return to this original concept of the profession, as the benefits of allowing one's skills to develop in this way are becoming increasingly clear. As our territory widens, the important thing is to straddle architecture and engineering while maintaining control: quantitatively, seeking the depths of each role, and qualitatively, integrating them and erasing the borders between them. From now on, the professional role of the architect will steadily change.

PROFESSIONAL SPECIALIZATION

This argument is not limited to engineering, but can also be applied to construction and project management. In the past, the professional role of the architect was to coordinate these consultants, but in our current age of information overload the professional field has deepened, and as time passes it becomes increasingly clear that there is a limit to what any one person is capable of achieving. Although the traditional image of the architect is that of a person who orchestrates individual experts in creating a work of architecture, it seems that under current conditions one must be content with the range of architecture that it is possible to grasp as an individual, unable to cope with the never-ending expansion of architectural thought and technology.

Architecture should be regarded from multiple viewpoints. When approached directly, at some point it will become necessary to find a system for dividing the field of architecture into various specializations. Within this system of division of labor, the convergence of various specialized technologies may be excellent. On the other hand, as identical technologies have become ubiquitous, their potentials can no longer be appreciated from the outside: the specialized fields have relinquished the possibility of entering one another, or alternatively, in their desperation at not being able to enter other fields have closed themselves off, protecting themselves from penetration by others. I am not suggesting that the division of labor is in itself a bad thing, but although there is a positive necessity for the division of labor, something must also be discarded in any given situation despite its advantages. Rather than abandoning specialization and attempting to do everything ourselves, the direction we must follow is to allow specialization while analyzing the benefits it provides for architecture. Maintaining the depth of our initial specialized knowledge, we must also attempt integration. We must not make the mistake of losing the advantages conferred by specialization. But neither will integration result in the loss of depth of knowledge.

SYNCHRONIZED COLLABORATION

I use the word *collaboration* to describe this feedback process of integrating specializations. Based on such collaboration, I expect that we will transcend our current era of overspecialization and the inability to share knowledge with one another. In other words, *synchronized collaboration* is an activation of the specific knowledge of all team members while aligning them all in the same direction. While it is impossible to impart 100% of one's knowledge to others, members of a design team can share the general outline of their knowledge with one another, and perhaps collaboration might then proceed through the simultaneous specialization and integration of knowledge. In order to access information that one is unaware of but might potentially be in the immediate vicinity, it is important to be open to outside influences. Perhaps one begins to change by first accepting the limits of one's own knowledge; one's own fundamental identity may be maintained, but synchronized collaboration is only possible if we are prepared to let go of our certainties.

I think of synchronized collaboration as a structure, in the general sense of the word. Each element = *material*, each relationship = *structure*, and results – the totality – are generated accordingly. The design process is constructed as a network structure, the extent of which is unknown. In cases where the design process is predicated on such a network structure, each member of the team becomes a single "material." What we know is merely one opinion, and feedback from other people opens us to possibilities we could never have imagined on our own. These possibilities are not to be found in a superficial comprehension of existing knowledge, but rather in a return to first principles, which may perhaps be achieved by simply linking the individual wills of all the people involved.

These do not need to be big things; even very small things may contain immense potential, and it is only due to the flukes of history that any one of our "new" discoveries is not already common knowledge. If this is true, the important thing is not what we think, but what we actually attempt to do.

THE LIMITATIONS OF LANGUAGE
When people hear a specific word, they are immediately contained within its frame. Escaping this is my main intention. I therefore think it would be a good idea to abandon the current system of division of labor, to remove the inherent limitations of words such as "architecture" and "engineering." I have been studying this conclusion for some time now, and I can say that what has begun to occur greatly exceeds my expectations. This potential is even now expanding within our society, no matter what my own opinion might be.

The important thing is to simply accept the facts of what occurs. The notion of *discovery* is not the making of new things, but the revelation of previously unnoticed aspects within what already exists. I call such a discovery *natural sense*: we uncover new possibilities one by one, and each fresh discovery, although it has not previously existed, seems obvious when found. It is not a special thing, just one that did not previously exist.

OBVIOUS "ART"
One consequence of this concept of discovery is that the border between technology and art is erased. The Japanese words for "technology/technique" (gijutsu) and "fine art" (geijutsu) may both be translated into English as "art". Because their original source is the same, perhaps this is obvious. I want to imply both meanings when I say "art": the simultaneous existence of art and technology, everyday technology and everyday art. It would be good if future technology follows this definition, to begin creating this previously nonexistent, obvious "art."

IMAGINARY STRUCTURE
The word structure implies a double meaning: *real* structure and *imaginary* structure. "Real structure" means the building components, structural members, insulation, surface finishes. "Imaginary structure" returns to my starting point: the elements composing architecture, materials and their interrelationships - a site, a person, a building, etc.
Within a design, thinking about a real structure is usually done in correspondence with the imaginary structure. If one has no knowledge of the real structure, the final result may come from consideration of the imaginary structure, but the reverse may also be true. These two types of structure are considered simultaneously. The important thing is that the various forms of knowledge generated from within several projects undertaken simultaneously always extend beyond each specific project, as feedback allowing knowledge to be exchanged among them.
I am currently interested in attempting to design under different simultaneous conditions. The following pages explain the relationships between the design process and these various conditions, using examples from projects I have recently been engaged in.

SENDAI MEDIATHEQUE
Site: Sendai, Japan. Building design: Toyo Ito. Structure design: SSC+MIAS

Here, I will only discuss the use of a double layer of Profilit glass in part of the exterior wall. We were initially told by the local glass maker, Nippon Sheet Glass (Mr. Seiji Ikeuchi and Mr. Masashi Kikuta), that the inner layer would not bear any of the wind load, and the outer layer acting alone would break when overstressed. Unfortunately, this meant that an intermediate horizontal beam was deemed necessary. The proof of this was demonstrated via nonlinear analysis.

Studying the problem led to the obvious suggestion (*natural sense*) of introducing a certain amount of air between the two layers of glass in order to provide some compensatory air pressure between inside and outside. Although at first everybody was uncertain, further examination led to the surprising discovery that air would be able to enter through an existing water drainage

hole in the outer layer of glass (which was ignored in the initial calculations). With some minor adjustments to this water drainage hole, the strength of the inner layer of glass would in fact be sufficient, and as a result, the intermediate beam could be eliminated without making any major changes.

See page 148

© Seiji Ikeuchi

NATURAL UNIT

Site: Kanagawa, Japan. Building design: EDH Endo Design Room + MIAS

This is a project done in collaboration with Masaki Endo, based on the theme of concrete. The project was realized by constantly checking each idea throughout the construction period, but delaying their final integration until the last possible moment.

A 10cm concrete wall was required for sound insulation, and it is simple and appropriate to make curved forms with cast concrete. Using steel members (acting as both structure and scaffolding) which varied incrementally in angle, it was possible to keep all the deckplates (acting as both formwork and finish) at the same width. Acoustic insulation was integrated with the deckplates; at the same time, the sound screening properties of the double glazed south facade were confirmed, and acoustic insulation was used in the ceiling on the interior of the double glass. The entire assemblage combines sound absorption, sound screening and structural properties. Additionally, the convex surface of the curved form results in very good acoustics. Because the clients happened to be a couple comprised of a pianist and an acoustics expert, this could be confirmed once the building was completed and the quantity and location of the sound absorbing materials were fixed. It was finally possible to use far less sound insulation than the calculations had indicated.

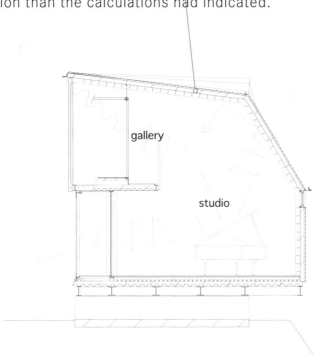

gallery

studio

AMBI-FLUX

Site: Tokyo, Japan. Building design: Architecton, MIAS

Located in the heart of Tokyo, this is an urban house typology. Its structure is based on a Miesian floor plan raised into the vertical plane: in other words, the vertical walls are structured using a grid of beams. This allows both the floors and walls to be located with the same freedom as random Miesian columns. The space is thereby created by two surfaces, and the flow of air through the large void is important. The electrical services are unified with the structure by locating them within the wall grid, and air circulates within the planar surfaces (floor and walls) linking the two column grids. It was necessary for the flow of air above and below to be unified with the structure. The layout of the planar surfaces (floors and walls) was defined by following the movement of people and air, and in fact this turned out to be identical to the layout required by the structural load paths. The design process proceeded with simultaneous development of the wall thicknesses, overall proportions and costs.

© Koji Okumura

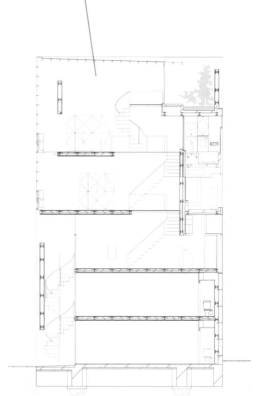

ROOF HOUSE

Site: Kanagawa, Japan. Building design: Tezuka Architects, MIAS

As the title shows, the most important element of this building is its roof. Based on the same plan, this could become a simple, single-storey house, depending on how the roof is executed.

This roof surface it is perceived neither as an ancient Japanese type of roof, nor one that utilizes high-tech, but carefully devised and assembled based on

existing technologies. This occurs not only above on the roof; when one passes through to below, a similar awareness occurs. Having abstracted the function of each architectural element, all that remained was this roof (or floor); by giving it a slight incline, the material of this final function was also successfully sublimated.

See page 272

SENSE AND COMMONSENSE

Sense is that which may be understood by only one person, while *commonsense* may be shared between many people. Within the genre of architecture, these two types of sense frequently encounter one another, yet all too often they cannot reach a compromise. How can we handle these two apparently opposed value systems? Perhaps in terms of the problem of technology.

SENSE OF BALANCE

When Renzo Piano gave the 7th Praemium Imperiale award memorial lecture in Japan in 1995, someone in the audience asked for his views on the relationship between architecture and technology. Piano replied by talking about a pianist who performs Chopin. To play Chopin means to engage the difficulty and beauty of his music. Imagine a pianist who wishes to play a difficult piece of music. With sufficient practice, it may be performed successfully. However, having achieved this, the pianist's level of expertise has increased, and they will then wish to attempt an even more difficult piece of music. Technology and architecture have a similar relationship, according to Piano; which one comes first is irrelevant.

In other words, image and technology are mutually linked. Images are not prioritized; rather, technology and images mutually enhance one another.

It is interesting that these two things (image and technology) step forward together, taking each other's hand and moving in the same direction. I believe the relationship of sense and commonsense may be regarded in a similar way: in other words, the two will eventually converge. This sense of balance is very personal; I became aware of it through working on real projects, and encountering these various senses.

I wish to somehow eliminate those things that are not part of either the architectural system or the structural system. For example, in some cases the quantity of cladding substrate is actually greater than that of the structural materials. So in one particular project the surface finish was eliminated, and in a subsequent project, the surface finish itself was incorporated within the structure and the substrate was eliminated. In this way, the very meaning of "structure", "substrate" or "surface finish" vanishes.

n another project, the substrate was left without a surface finish, and we moved directly to studying the details. The safety of a building depends more on its details than on the size and number of its structural members: just through developing them, the safety factor may be increased many times over. The structure disappears, leaving only the substrate.

n yet another project, this concept was further developed. After studying ways of making the construction process easier, the structural members were divided so they were each of a weight manageable by human strength. The builders looked at the system and said there was no cladding, while the building permit office said there is no structure. Which statement is actually correct? It doesn't really matter, since we were not designing with the intention of creating labels. The important thing is that the architecture is organised technologically, the exterior resists the climate, living within it is comfortable, and consensus is achieved amongst the people involved.

Many similar events have occurred often over the last few years. As a gradual accumulation of minor things, it has been interesting to see the way a variety of results may be developed from a single starting point. The same thing can never be created a second time. The solution will change each time as various people communicate. It is interesting to be involved in the design of a house, as various architectural essences may be identified over a relatively brief time period. We quickly try one idea, then another... I cherish this method of collaboration. This is because my individual sense is exposed to the senses of others, and these exchanges apply commonsense to the effects of our individual senses upon one another.

ECONOMY

To make something that does not depend on money requires a very wide layer of support. It is via commonsense that its value is recognised in the wider world, and I do not ignore this when designing. This does not mean choosing cheap surface finishes; by analysing each system we may find their shared, repetitive components and thereby turn them into an integrated system. Cost performance is improved from a very small initial viewpoint.

For example, in the case of a building with a reinforced concrete structure, we tried to eliminate the formwork. Formwork is a significant percentage of the cost, and becomes industrial waste after construction is finished. It is very useful to think about such simple problems. This is not just for construction; such studies must be repeated by every member of the team - the experts in design, construction or acoustics. Here, concrete was given the additional function of soundproofing. The curved form and the potential of concrete to assume a variety of shapes were unified. Finally, the steel formwork also became the surface finish. There is no waste, and no inconvenience to the other elements.

It is also important to become involved with ordinary construction techniques. Even with the same result, cost is affected by the construction process.

This can be understood by observation on site, and from there many ideas originate. Therefore, I am present on site as much as possible. It is important to consult people directly. Depending on which individuals you meet, the process will be altered.

Having been achieved once, a particular technique may also be passed on to others. I do not want to use a particular idea only once, but as much as possible reuse it in other projects. By using the wisdom of others without relying on habitual techniques, the quantity of materials can be reduced and cost performance improved, a desirable goal with great potential.

SAFETY

I doubt anyone would disagree that safety is as much commonsense as the issue of economic efficiency. Particularly since the Kobe (Great Hanshin) earthquake in Japan, the attention paid by clients to safety issues has increased. The feeling at that time and since is that there are subtle differences between the perceptions of safety by the client, those stipulated by the building code, and those determined by the designers' ethical standards. So although the client may not fully understand why, he believes that the building he has personally commissioned is safe; this is because the building permit office only declares that it is safe if it is designed within the scope of the law, and when it is outside that scope, it is not approved. This kind of implicit understanding must occur far more within "commonsense."

I always begin by trying to consider things qualitatively rather than quantitatively. Within the world of engineering, numerical proofs are always based on certain hypotheses, and it could be said that most conditions are hypothetical. It is therefore important to think about engineering at a conceptual level rather than just as calculations, a difference we could describe as similar to that between analog and digital. It is possible to deceive people who do not understand engineering by mathematical tricks, but if one does not understand it, escaping the limits of commonsense is difficult. By analyzing a phenomenon and breaking it down into parts, its potential may be revealed. For example, considering the earthquake-prone nature of Japan, I intend to continue investigating lightweight construction. If the weight of something subject to an earthquake is halved, its earthquake energy is also halved. This is obvious when the phenomenon is reconsidered.

I make a point of explaining this because it is easier to adapt to unpredicted situations if they are considered qualitatively, and actual safety may be hugely improved rather than just calculated safety factors. Take a substance like steel. It is relatively strong and so has relatively thin components. It therefore becomes necessary to take into account the phenomenon of buckling: when force is constantly applied, it will suddenly buckle. On the other hand, the construction as a whole is resistant to bending. In reconsidering such a phenomenon, I always try to construct the whole by adjusting it to the respective characteristics of the material. When I consider a steel construction in terms of its members (columns) taking compressive loads, I generally consider two techniques. When it is desirable to make the columns thin, they are placed at close intervals; if wide spans are acceptable, I try to eliminate the columns themselves. In the former case, by using many columns, in the rare incident that one buckles, the surrounding columns will take the extra load. In the world of safety as defined by probability theory, dispersion causes variation to decrease, and the safety factor then greatly increases. On the other hand, in cases where there are no adjacent members to assist and the loads are borne by the members that constitute the floor and roof, the *actual* safety factor increases because the bending phenomenon is far slower than the buckling phenomenon, so the structure will gradually deform without suddenly breaking.

NATURAL SENSE

There is another type of sense, which I call *natural sense*. It differs from the present sense of balance in that it is no longer individual, but may be shared. In other words, it is the sense that originates where the boundary between sense and commonsense becomes ambiguous: while it is very personal, it is also possible to share with others.

Natural sense is the sensation that occurs when unpredictable conditions appear before one's eyes, born from synchronized collaboration due to the technique of imaginary structure. It is an unprecedented yet obvious perception. We cannot predict what it will lead to. Perhaps it may be possible to sense it in the completed construction. In other words, it is not an image which standardizes the whole, but something which is born from the accumulation of parts, the result of minor things.

If newly invented things are not an improvement over currently existing things, it would be better to do nothing at all. For example, if it is not unreasonable for a particular architectural idea to be realized using currently available ordinary technologies, then it would be meaningless to use a higher level of technology. This is not a bad thing; it truly is sufficient. When a new type of architecture is to be invented, it makes sense to develop new technology. Architecture and technology must therefore be linked and upgraded in tandem. Neither takes precedence. This is the expectation of natural sense.

Therefore, in the world of architecture, the borders of design, structure, equipment and construction are exceeded, and design must progress via feedback and synchronized collaboration. From this conflict unprecedented things may emerge, but which might be obvious architectural solutions from every viewpoint.

ALMERE STADTSTHEATER
Site: Almere, Netherlands. Building design: SANAA. Structure design: SSC + MIAS, ABT

In Japan, we have realised many steel sandwich roof structures. In this case, as a preliminary experiment, steel sandwich structural walls were proposed. These could probably be executed without difficulty in Japan; in the Netherlands, this was converted into a structural system using steel plate walls and a concrete roof for cost reasons. It is extremely interesting that changes were made in materials and construction processes while maintaining the essence of the construction system and satisfying the demands of both cost and design. In the actualization of these changes, probably the most important factor was a series of meetings in which the project managers, the end users and all the consultants reevaluated the cost estimates, through the practical and flexible interaction of the entire team.

As a result, I gained the impression that although the starting points may be identical, the development process is very different in Japan and the Netherlands. Particularly here in Europe, where the history of concrete architecture originated in France, replacing the steel roof system with a flat concrete slab seems like a very natural solution in retrospect. Furthermore, there is the issue of sound insulation, and assuming a very large roof load, the substitution with concrete was very advantageous. If this was done again in Europe under different initial conditions, we would probably reach a different solution.

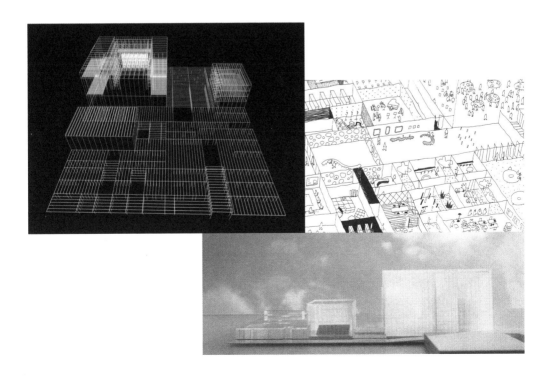

TOLEDO MUSEUM OF ART

Site: Toledo, USA. Building design: SANAA. Structure design: SPAS + MIAS, GNA

As in Almere, a roof with a steel sandwich structure was proposed. In the US, even members with very large sections are available preformed, so these were used rather than going to the trouble of welding. In this way, the lower plate of the sandwich panel was removed, and large I-beams were attached to the upper steel plate instead. The essential structural system was not changed, just altered to correspond with the local industries.

The system of division of labor is particularly well-established in America. The task of project manager is therefore very important. Furthermore, from the basic design stage onwards, there were frequent staff meetings with quantity surveyors and various consultants, and the change in the structural system was a realistic method of lowering costs.

Because this is a fairly cold area (as in Almere), thermal insulation was necessary in order to lower energy consumption. It was interesting to discover that energy consumption is quite low despite the glazed facade, because in this characteristically flat SANAA building the majority of the surface area is roof and foundation.

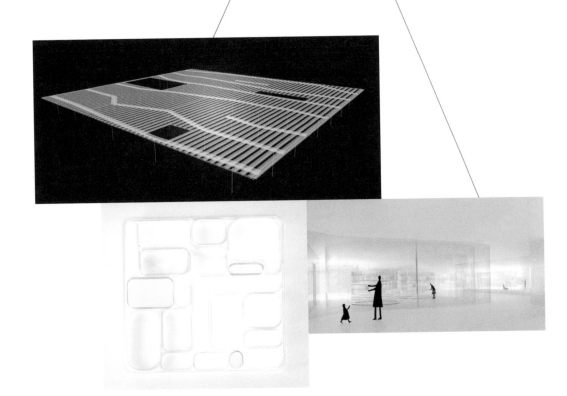

RELAXATION PARK

Site: Torrevieja, Spain. Building design: Toyo Ito. Structure design: SAPS + MIAS, OMA

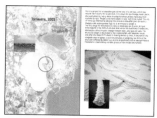

See page 188

The keyword for this project was "spiral." The eastern Mediterranean region of Spain is similar to the Japanese monsoon climate, and the design process itself was also quite Japanese. Because earthquakes occur very infrequently in comparison with Japan, the conditions are considerably easier here.

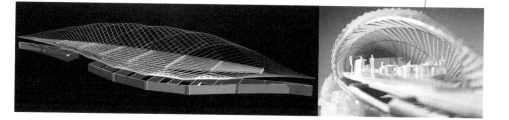

MATSUDAI CULTURAL CENTER

Site: Matsudai, Japan. Building design: MVRDV + SUPER-OS + CLIP. Structure design: SAPS + MIAS

Although the architects are Dutch, this project is located in Japan. The viewpoint is reversed. I was impressed by the way Dutch architects are willing to completely alter the design in an instant, even when it has reached a fairly advanced stage, as a practical solution to functional and budget problems. They well understand when it is necessary to abandon an idea.

Despite its bold form, the building has a very good scale relationship to its site. Visitors during winter will enter the snow-covered passages then suddenly emerge into the main space. The building became a pure example of the numerically-based architectural concepts of MVRDV, unifying construction and form. Being built by Japanese contractors, it seems that even the finer details will be well-executed.

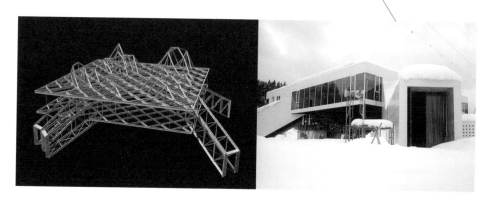

MATSUNOYAMA NATURAL SCIENCE MUSEUM

Site: Matsunoyama, Japan. Building design: Tezuka Architects, MIAS

This project is located in Matsunoyama, a city neighboring Matsudai, and takes into consideration Japan's harsh natural environment. The scale, budget, program and producer are the same. As in Matsudai, this area is at times covered by 4 or 5 meters of snow. In Matsudai, the building is raised above the magnificent drifts of snow to a height of 6 meters, but in Matsunoyama, it is firmly embedded in the land, burrowed into the snow and awaiting the thaw. From within it becomes possible to sense the light filtered by snow via enormous acrylic-covered openings.

The external walls are made of structural Corten steel, and there are no eaves to protect against the winter snows. It is a monolithic structure with strong ribs

inside to withstand the enormous snow loads. During the summer, the 160m long volume may move and twist in order to cope with thermal deformation caused by direct sunlight raising the surface temperature. This undulating shape can be imagined as actually winding itself around a number of fulcrums.

See page 258

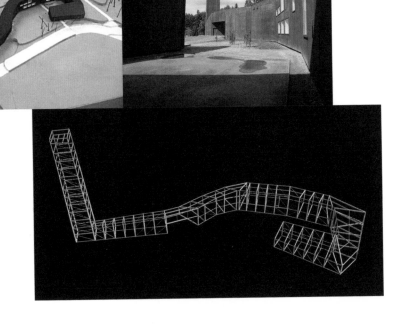

ORIGINAL FIGURE: A FIGURE WHICH GRADUALLY BECOMES VISIBLE AS THE EYES ARE CLOSED

The word *figure* expresses both internal structure and external form. The point of using this word in contrast with general terms such as shape and form is that it captures the total character, including the interior. This is profoundly different from just talking about outward appearance: it implies the delicate nuances of continuity between interior space and exterior form, and their becoming a single entity.

The word "figure" might be appropriate to describe an architecture (or any aspect of culture) in which the external form emerges in unity with the internal structure. In architecture, internal structure is related to the various phenomena of the architectural process, something which cannot be grasped only visually (this is what I call imaginary structure). We architects must now decide how to best convey this architectural "figure" to the public, for our own benefit and for people involved in other forms of cultural activity.

It has become an acknowledged fact that in photographs, texts and even detailed drawings, the more the quantity and accuracy of information is increased, the more things are lost. Only through intense reading of the context does this "figure" start to become visible. I would like to capture the moment at which the figure shows its shape. It is the moment that something inside me becomes architecture. It is probably therefore necessary to raise one's consciousness in order to be able to select from the overflow of information, without being misled by commonly accepted stereotypes. If our level of consciousness is raised, we begin to see the same things differently. In other words, we must all be sensors, highly aware at all times.

Everything has a virtual existence prior to becoming actualized, and this is the *original figure*. As one slowly closes one's eyes, redundant elements gradually vanish. Although everything seems linked, the relationships of where and how they are connected become unclear. However, this is in fact their origin, perhaps even their fundamental essence. Each person must discover this original figure for themselves, by trial and error. This original figure is something like a judgment standard, or perhaps a directional vector. Without this, no matter how many highly-aware sensors we have, we will drown in the deluge of information.

Toyo Ito
Barcelona, 2003

By now everybody knows the story of the Sendai Mediatheque. (For a complete account of the building's history, see *Verb*'s monograph, *Sendai Mediatheque*). Here we present a more personal account from Toyo Ito, where he talks about the relation of the Mediatheque to his ideas of permanence and impermanence: how something as solid and final as the matter of architecture can also be used to prolong the instability and 'in-completeness' of a building. This interview was conducted by Kelly Shannon and Tom Avermaete on 22nd. February 2000, while the Mediatheque was in the process of construction.

Tom Avermaete Your continuing fascination with 'primitive bodies' (man's natural state) as contrasted to 'virtual bodies' (the contemporary condition where the body is a receptacle for electronic flows) is highlighted in the Mediatheque, which was envisioned as a new prototype for a structure where these two bodies can integrate. What are the limits to breaking down the conventional relationship between architecture/city/space and the human body? Will the physical containers of human activity continue to be framed by the social institution 'architecture' or are the opportunities of information technology eradicating the need for architecture?

Toyo Ito I have been talking about these two bodies for quite a long time. How to integrate them is a question which also includes certain fundamental contradictions; it is not a paradox that can easily be solved.
I define our virtual body as it links to the world of information, something which I used to refer to in terms of telephone, fax, these kinds of media. But in the last few years this tendency has grown stronger and the relationship more complex due to developments in information technology. On the one hand people have e-mail addresses, communication devices which reduce or erase distances, but the 'primitive body' is still in its original condition. On the one hand it may seem that the distinction between public and private space is disappearing, like the ability to have private conversations in a public space with mobile phones. On the other hand, there is a sense of isolation in people using these phones

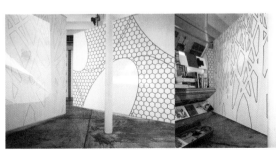

being connected with somebody very far away... In a certain way globalization is completely parallel to isolation. We are not living in the same 'place', but there are still huge distances. So I want to try to postpone this isolation, or at least make it more vague.

I am facing the same situation in the Sendai Mediatheque project; the same paradox is present. One of the tasks we faced was to provide a space that would be agreeable and easy to use, as comfortable as possible for people to enter the Internet – the virtual space. Here the gap between the two bodies became very clear, more clear then ever.

Kelly Shannon What is the newness in the Mediatheque prototype?

TI The space of Mediatheque is very homogeneous, a bit like the Dom-ino system of Le Corbusier. One big difference with Le Corbusier is that it makes use of tubes that support the structure, which are hollow and bend like trees, which are not positioned at equal distances but are randomly spread.

I wanted to reintroduce the idea of mobility and fluidity into the space, to express the fact that there is always something streaming through the building, as a metaphor for the stream of information. I also wanted to express that because of this stream, the architecture allows for different programming and changes: there is no fixed center, no hierarchy. It has been five years now since we won the competition, and so far I have been able to prevent the tubes from separating the building into small parts, into separate rooms. Maybe not in a perfect way, but to a certain extent I have been able to build spaces that are not limited, that can serve people and thus are both served and servant spaces.

The newness of the Mediatheque is also in the four programs that are integrated in the project. I think that we can talk about a certain mixture of programs and spaces, despite the problems we had with local authorities and codes. The library system in Japan is a very rigid one. It is very hard to break it up, to find cracks in the system and do something new. We have been in discussion for 5 years about the hard elements of the construction, but also about how to organize the program, and I think we have made some progress.

KS You have spoken of your buildings as being continually 'under construction', as well as of the difference between 'hard' and 'soft' construction in architecture.

TI 'Hard construction' means the physical process of construction of architecture. Over two years I have been struggling, fighting with the steel construction elements on the construction site in Sendai. This was a construction site where I was confronted more then ever before with steel and the fusing of steel, the merging of steel…
 'Soft construction' means the process of making programmed spaces out of that construction. Hard construction finishes at a certain point in time, and we begin to use the building, but if the space is served flexibly enough, the program itself can continue to change. The ideal situation would be that our idea of construction would not relate only to the solid, physical part of architecture that finishes at a certain time, so that this condition of being 'under construction' can continue even after the building has been built.
In this sense the plans and sections of the Mediatheque are simply the results or examples of what we have been discussing for the last five years. I want to express that architecture is continuously changing in this sense. Of course the solid physical part has to be contained within a clearly delimited space – for example the air conditioning has to work, it has to be closed off – but the plans, the actual design, are still to be written. In this way I want to avoid it becoming a sort of complete or perfect type of building, to avoid that it becomes completely frozen or 'finished'.

TA What are the instruments for an architect to avoid a building becoming frozen and finished?

TI The competition entry for the Mediatheque was nothing more than a very schematic plan of floors, tubes and facades. In this way I wanted to express that I would not like it to become a frozen thing. But at a certain point there came a moment when the building had to have walls, to have protection from the elements and a physical demarcation between inside and outside. So I used a different treatment of the façades to make the cut visible between the building and the outside. Every plane has a different outlook: the front façade is made of double glazing, the side became steel-plated because it had to integrate emergency stairs, the roof is a grid. The floor heights also vary, so there is a certain interchangeability between the floors. I wanted to express how a space which should have been, in a vertical as well as a horizontal way, much more open to the environment, is cut off in this manner because of necessity.

TA Does this mean that you consider the process of materializing architecture an unavoidable ending point, a negative point, because the process of change stops?

TI It is not an easy fact for me to acknowledge that what was initially conceived as something open and 'in process' suddenly has to be finished or cut off. As long as I remain within the realm of architecture, I cannot avoid the transformation of an open-ended concept into built form through materialization and communication with society. Nonetheless, I still carry in me the hope to become free of these limitations, and that is why I turn to computer graphics.

Jaime Salazar CAD and some architects' thinking are evolving very quickly, but building practices are not. Designing and building practices have no correspondence; this seems to be the great paradigm to solve now. Materiality in architecture is, of course, very much related to a certain construction industry and a market which does not easily accept changes; architects like Greg Lynn and Ben van Berkel try to move beyond the present forms of architectural materiality but still have to face, even in the most advanced countries, anachronistic building practices. As such, the architectural debate about 'boxes' (pre-computerized structures) versus 'blobs' (computer-aided structures) has no meaning at present: architects have tools to design 'blobs' but hardly have ways to build them. MVRDV, for example, says that they design 'boxes' not because they cannot conceive of 'blobs', but because the building industry isn't capable of materializing them. Is Japan making the first steps towards another kind of fluid computerized relationship between design and construction data?

TI Japan is no different than the rest of the world in its use of the computer in architecture; there is no real step towards something new in the relation between the two. I do not like idea of a contradiction between people who design and people who construct buildings. It is more that people who design things have, at a certain point and through communication with their social surroundings, to try to realize their projects. But I also do not think the problem of blobs and boxes will be solved purely by technology in the future, because our bodies also have this gap between the two, and architectural space still has to accept these bubble-bodies. So my interests are in how I can accept and express this contradiction.

The situation in Japan is exactly the same as anywhere else. It is possible to make very nice models on the computer, but architecture will always involve separating inside from outside. When it comes to the stage of creating the building, it is unavoidable. A lot of problems relate to this establishing of the border between inside and outside; the details, the choice of materials and so on. I respond by trying make this border between inside and outside as blurred, as unclear, as possible. It is not possible to eradicate the distinction completely because that would imply leaving the realm of architecture.

KS Do you consider this blurring as a future project for architecture?

TI I do not know if this is a tendency that is going to be very general. My interest is in that field, there is no more to it. Concerning this question I cannot say that I am optimistic or pessimistic.

KS Are you optimistic for the future of the profession?

TI If I were not optimistic I would be obliged to stop.

Sendai,
150 minutes northeast of Tokyo

As Toyo Ito says, there is a parallel between natural flows and information flows, and so these are naturally related in his buildings. The tubes of the Mediatheque developed from ideas about the transmission of structural and informational flows through the building, but also from the image of seaweed floating in water. The façade of the Tod's store (see page 202) returns to the web-like structure of the Mediatheque and the Serpentine pavilion, but is directly generated from overlapping patterns of zelkova trees. So Ito's work involves the same ideas about natural and informational networks that this issue of *Verb* is all about.

12. 05. 1998　　03. 07. 1998　　19. 08. 1998　　02. 09. 1998　　22. 10. 1998

04. 08. 1999　　07. 09. 1999　　25. 11. 1999　　23. 12. 1999　　27. 01. 2000

SKETCH BY TOYO ITO (COMPETITION PHASE)

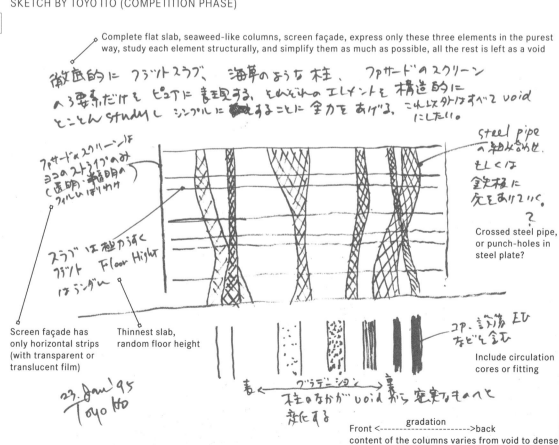

Complete flat slab, seaweed-like columns, screen façade, express only these three elements in the purest way, study each element structurally, and simplify them as much as possible, all the rest is left as a void

徹底的に フラットスラブ、 海草のような 柱、 ファサードのスクリーン へ3要素だけを ピュアに 表現する、 とんぞれの エレメントを 構造的に とことん study し シンプルに する ことに 全力をあげる。これ以外はすべて void にしたい。

steel pipe の組み合わせ、 もしくは 鉄板に 欠をあけていく。 ?

Crossed steel pipe, or punch-holes in steel plate?

ファサードのスクリーンは ヨコの ストライプ へのみ (透明・半透明の フィルムばりわけ

Screen façade has only horizontal strips (with transparent or translucent film)

スラブは極力うすく フラット Floor Hight はランダム

Thinnest slab, random floor height

コア、設備 など を 全む

Include circulation cores or fitting

23. Jan '95
Toyo Ito

表 ← グラデーション → 裏 柱のなかが void から 密実なものへと 変化する

Front <————gradation————> back
content of the columns varies from void to dense

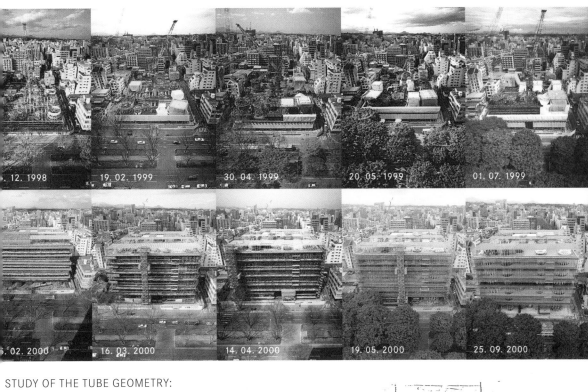

. 12. 1998   19. 02. 1999   30. 04. 1999   20. 05. 1999   01. 07. 1999

. 02. 2000   16. 03. 2000   14. 04. 2000   19. 05. 2000   25. 09. 2000

STUDY OF THE TUBE GEOMETRY:
SKETCH BY MUTSURO SASAKI (COMPETITION PHASE)

TUBES

TUBE COORDINATES PLANS

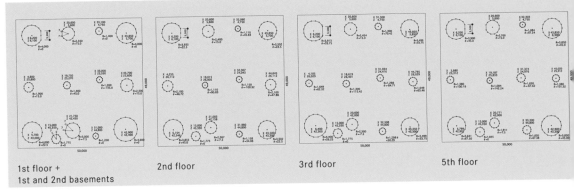

1st floor +
1st and 2nd basements

2nd floor

3rd floor

5th floor

TUBE ASSEMBLY

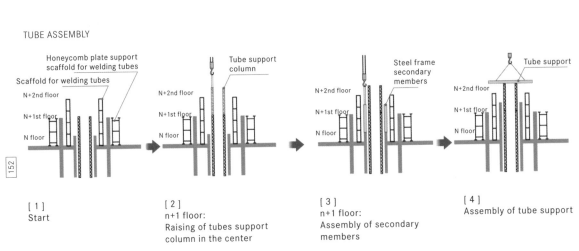

[1]
Start

[2]
n+1 floor:
Raising of tubes support
column in the center

[3]
n+1 floor:
Assembly of secondary
members

[4]
Assembly of tube support

© Dana Buntrock

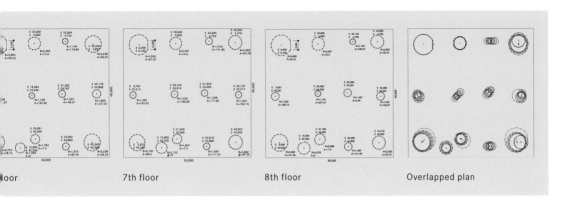

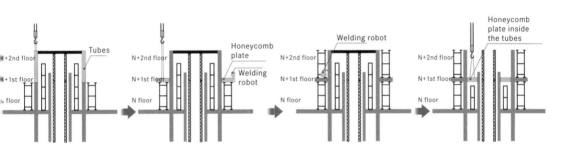

| loor | 7th floor | 8th floor | Overlapped plan |

[ ]
1 floor:
sembly of tubes

[6]
n+1 floor:
Assembly and welding
of honeycomb plates

[7]
n+1 floor:
Welding of tube joints

[8]
n+1 floor:
Assembly the honeycomb
plates inside the tube

long vinyl tile t=30mm
including mortar
aluminium non-slip

stairs hanger: PC steel bar
φ=32mm UP

heat shield glass t=15mm fire proof sash

float glass t=12mm
with silk printed film

fire door

6F tube ring: hard fire proofing
t=15mm UP on FR steel

flooring t=12mm
impregnant paint
structural plywood t=9mm
OA floor 500x500mm t=23mm
dust protective paint
structural lightweight concrete

▼6FL : GL+21,655

**heat shield glass
t=15mm fire proof sash**

fire resistive covering:
rock wool spraying t=30+5mm
clearance for equipment
lightweight steel frame ceiling
substrate t=38+19mm
plaster board t=9.5+9.5 mm

rib: tempered glass t=19mm
with shatterproof film

float glass t=10mm
with silk printed film

flooring t=12mm
impregnant paint
structural plywood t=9mm
OA floor 500x500mm t=23mm
dust protective paint
structural lightweight concrete

fire door

▼5FL : GL+17,455

5F tube ring: hard fire proofing
t=15mm UP on FR steel

clearance for equipment
lightweight steel frame ceiling substrate
t=38+19mm
plaster board t=12.5mm robber
plaster board t=12.5mm elastic lithin spraying

heat shield glass t=21mm fire proof sash

rib: tempered glass t=19mm
with shatterproof film

float glass t=12mm
with silk printed film

fire door

▼4FL : GL+14,160

carpet t=10mm
OA floor 500x500mm t=23mm
dust protective paint
structural lightweight concrete

▼3FL : GL+11,450

3F tube ring: hard fire proofing
t=25mm UP on FR steel

heat shield glass t=15mm fire proof sash

fire resistive covering:
rock wool spraying t=45+5mm
glass wool t=25mm
clearance for equipment
lighting duct t=30mm
lightweight steel frame ceiling t=38mm
folded steel louver t=400 mm

vinyl tiles for double floor
500x500mm t=5mm
OA floor 500x500mm t=23mm
dust protective paint
structural lightweight concrete

rib: tempered glass t=19mm
with shatterproof film

float glass t=10mm
with silk printed film

fire door

▼2FL : GL+7,480

2F tube ring: fireproof painting
UP on FR steel

**structural steel
plate : FR steel UP**

rib: tempered glass t=19+12mm
with shatterproof film

long vinyl tile t=30mm
including mortar
aluminium non-slip

handrail cover: polyvinyl φ=34mm
baluster: steel φ=12mm

heat shield glass t=15mm
fire proof sash

bridge board (both sides)=steel FB-16x260mm

stair post: steel φ=216.3mm t=15.1mm

stair stringer: SUS plate t=25mm

fire door

marble t=20mm
base mortar t=45mm
slab: reinforced concrete t=150mm
deck plate: h=50mm

▼1FL : GL+20

35,480
5,490
CH=4,225
4,200
CH=3,295
31,825
3,295
2,710
CH=5,005
3,970
CH=2,906
7,460
CH=6,780

UNFOLDED GLASS PLAN

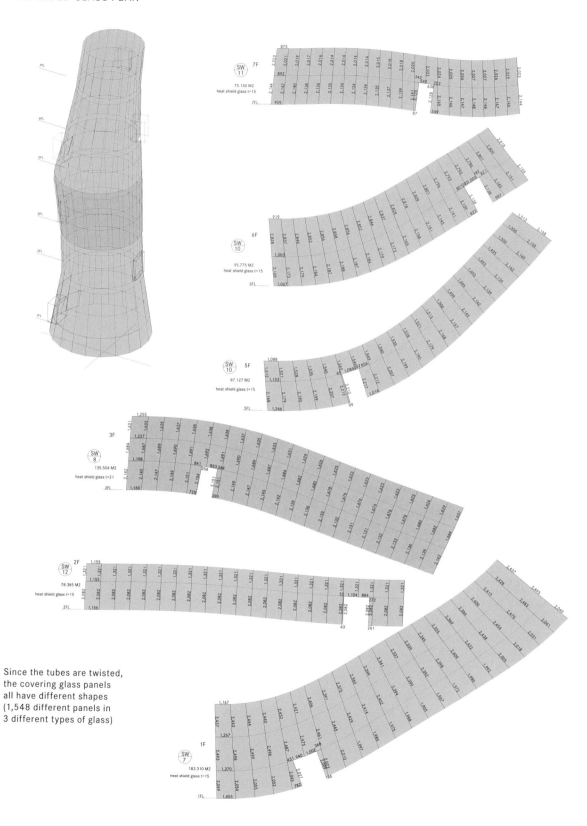

Since the tubes are twisted,
the covering glass panels
all have different shapes
(1,548 different panels in
3 different types of glass)

FAÇADE

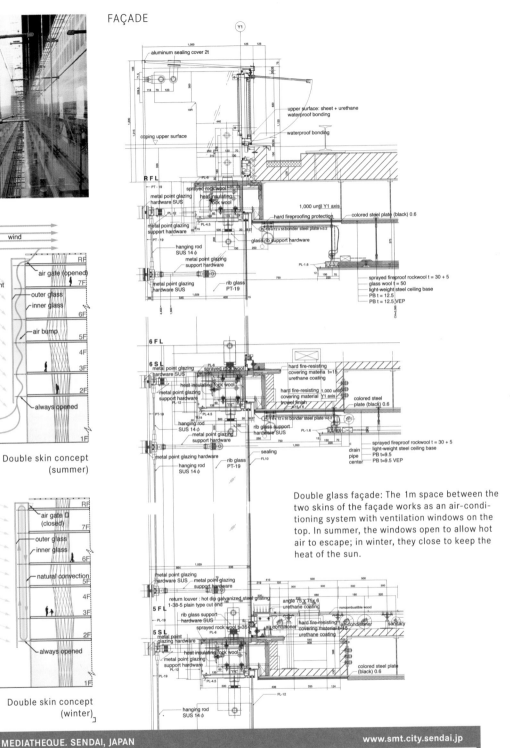

aluminum sealing cover 2t

upper surface: sheet + urethane waterproof bonding

waterproof bonding

coping upper surface

R F L

PT-19

metal point glazing hardware SUS

sprayed rock wool

heat insulating rock wool

1,000 until Y1 axis

hard fireproofing protection

colored steel plate (black) 0.6

metal point glazing support hardware

hanging rod SUS 14 φ

metal point glazing support hardware

glass rib support hardware

metal point glazing hardware SUS

rib glass PT-19

sprayed fireproof rockwool t = 30 + 5
glass wool t = 50
light-weight steel ceiling base
PB t = 12.5
PB t = 12.5 VEP

6 F L

6 S L

metal point glazing hardware SUS

sprayed rock wool

heat insulating rock wool

hard fire-resisting covering materia t=15 urethane coating

hard fire-resisting covering material trowel finish

1,000 until Y1 axis

colored steel plate (black) 0.6

metal point glazing support hardware

hanging rod SUS 14 φ

metal point glazing support hardware

rib glass support hardware SUS

metal point glazing hardware

sealing

hanging rod SUS 14 φ

rib glass PT-19

sprayed fireproof rockwool t = 30 + 5
light-weight steel ceiling base
PB t=9.5
PB t=9.5 VEP

drain pipe center

metal point glazing hardware SUS

metal point glazing support hardware

return louver : hot dip galvanized steel grating
1-38-5 plain type cut end

angle 75 X 75x 6
urethane coating

noncombustible wood

rib glass support hardware SUS

sprayed rock wool t=35

5 F L

5 S L

metal point glazing hardware

hard fire-resisting covering material t=15 urethane coating

air conditioner

sanitary

metal point glazing support hardware

heat insulating rock wool

colored steel plate (black) 0.6

hanging rod SUS 14 φ

Double glass façade: The 1m space between the two skins of the façade works as an air-conditioning system with ventilation windows on the top. In summer, the windows open to allow hot air to escape; in winter, they close to keep the heat of the sun.

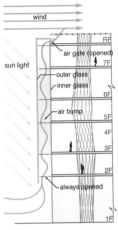

wind

sun light

RF
7F
air gate (opened)
outer glass
inner glass
6F
air bump
5F
4F
3F
2F
always opened
1F

Double skin concept (summer)

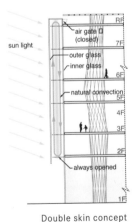

sun light

RF
7F
air gate (closed)
outer glass
inner glass
6F
natural convection
5F
4F
3F
2F
always opened
1F

Double skin concept (winter)

MEDIATHEQUE. SENDAI, JAPAN   www.smt.city.sendai.jp

Architects: Toyo Ito & Associates, Architects. Cost: 12,466,650,000 ¥. Area: site area 3,948.72 m², building area 2,933.12 m², total floor area 21,682.15 m², building height 36.49 m. Competition: 1994, design phase: 1995-1997, construction: 1997-2000, completion: 2000, opening: 2001. Client: Sendai City. Project member: Toyo Ito & Associates, Architects: Toyo Ito, Tatsuo Kuwahara, Takeo Higashi, Makoto Yokomizo, Toyohiko Kobayashi, Shinichi Takeuchi, Takuhiro Seo, Hironori Matsubara, Reo Yokota. Engineers: Sasaki Structural Consultants: Mutsuro Sasaki, Masahiro Ikeda, Shuji Tada, Akira Suzuki.

'Hungry horse' welding distortion on honeycomb slab ceiling

Ground floor: Entrance

Half-assembled tubes from the factory

Ground floor: Plaza

Deformed tubes allow access to the elevator

Second floor: Information Center

Finishing phase of construction

Third floor: Library

Brugge, 20:02 / 20.02.2002

Bruges Pavillion > Toyo Ito & Associates, Architects

The city of Bruges in Belgium, a beautiful city of medieval streets and canals, was European Cultural Capital in 2002. This project was for a pavilion that was intended to remain in the city's main square for just that one year.

Like any other old city, Bruges faces a potential conflict in its need to conserve its historic district while exploiting its potential as a modern city. Here we were requested to present a new architecture in the setting of the old town, with no specific function beyond symbolising the city's status as Cultural Capital.

Set against the city of stone, we proposed a tunnel-shaped aluminum honeycomb pavilion. Because the structure was too fragile to stand on its own, it was reinforced with patch-like aluminum panels on both surfaces, but only where absolutely

necessary. The panels were fitted at separate points with the loads between them distributed by the aluminum honeycomb which forms the outer shell of the structure. Despite being the result of very precise calculations based on structural analysis, the appearance is one of a spontaneous cutout picture.

A floating vitreous bridge spans a pond, an allusion to the foundations of a medieval church buried here some 50-60 centimetres underground. After that, the semi-transparent aluminum frame was carefully set on the bridge to complete the pavilion. Thus a semi-transparent object dotted with opaque elliptical patches, recalling the traditional lacework of Bruges, emerged from the water in the square surrounded by building facades in various styles.

The project began with a study of the structure. The honeycomb tube cannot resist the weight of an empty glass, but the same tube only partially covered with sandwich panels support can resist a full glass of water.

A MECHANICAL CUTOUT PICTURE A sketch by the engineer Masato Araya in the first phase of the project was quite impressive. It was drawn in response to the question: is it possible to make a structure of aluminum honeycomb mesh supported only by a pattern of "floating" patches? The load flow, usually calculated on a two-dimensional section diagram (moment diagram), was determined here on a model of the structural surface and converted into graphic patterns. The result was the network of interdependent floating panels that completes the structure of the construction. The various forms, looking like something out of a child's cutout picture, were drawn during meetings with the engineer. In deciding the form of the patches, there was a certain degree of freedom, constrained by the fact that any given form would require a different position and size.

A paper model was made first, followed by an aluminum model at 1:2 scale built in the garage of the studio.

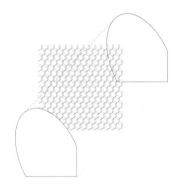

Thin aluminum panels
can support the unstable
aluminum honeycomb, as
a composite construction
material.

The light aluminum structure of the pavilion shows that new architecture can be integrated in historical scenes. The exterior is covered by transparent polycarbonate. Aluminum patterns float on the round pond, reflecting the shape of the foundations of the Roman cathedral which lay underground, and relating to the traditional laces of Brugge.

MODEL / EXPERIMENT / SIMULATION Since we were using materials and a structure unknown to us, we made a series of paper and aluminum models at various scales for the purpose of simulating and testing the structure. The size of each of these structural elements, the form of the floating patches and their pattern, and the manner of supporting the skins had direct bearing on the structural strength and visual appearance, so the process of making models in the studio also assumed an aspect of experimentation. In the final design phase, we made a 1:2 scale aluminum model. Around the same time, the model of the roof panel was made at a factory in Belgium. Based upon the results of these experiments, we changed the size of members. But we found it impossible to test the performance of the entire structural complex with a partial model, and thus made a full-scale model.

Each of the paper and aluminum models resembled the actual pavilion. Conceptually, the design process is endless, so the completed building was, in a broad sense, another in a series of models. Here the construction had no real function, so we could have relatively homogeneous patches. But if we imagine the pavilion at a different site or for a different activity, the patches would likely vary more in form.

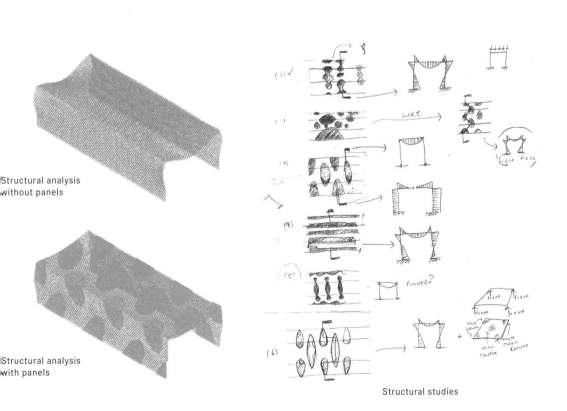

Structural analysis
without panels

Structural analysis
with panels

Structural studies

Plan

Aluminum plate
for welding oval

Weld

12

Hole on the oval (lower side) d=12

Stainless cap d=12

Honeycomb aluminum panel t=3

Datum point

Aluminum cylinder d=20
with female screw d=12

Center point

Hole on the oval (upper side) d=25

Section

Hole d=20

Stainless cap d=35

Polycarbonate t=12

12

30-48

Stainless ring d=20 t=1

Hole on the oval d=25

3

Aluminum cylinder d=20
with female screw d=8

125

Screw d=12

3

Oval: aluminum plate t=3

Hole on the oval d=12

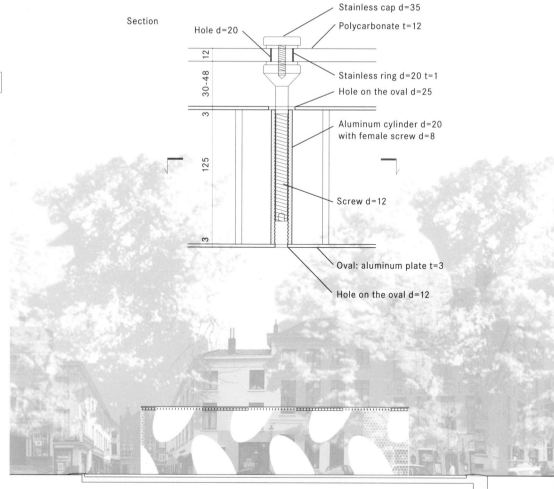

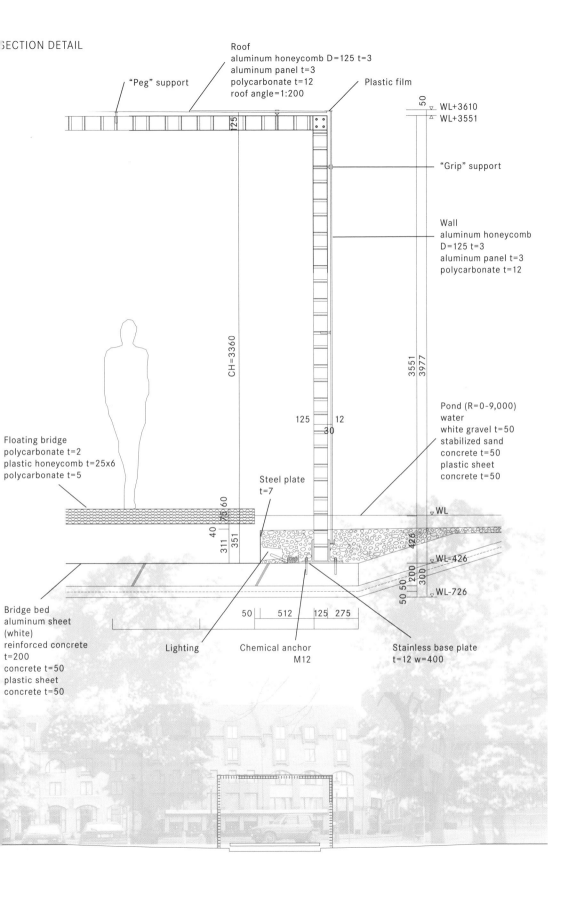

SECTION DETAIL

"Peg" support

Roof
aluminum honeycomb D=125 t=3
aluminum panel t=3
polycarbonate t=12
roof angle=1:200

Plastic film

50
▽ WL+3610
△ WL+3551

125

"Grip" support

Wall
aluminum honeycomb
D=125 t=3
aluminum panel t=3
polycarbonate t=12

CH=3360

3551
3977

Floating bridge
polycarbonate t=2
plastic honeycomb t=25×6
polycarbonate t=5

125   12
30

Pond (R=0-9,000)
water
white gravel t=50
stabilized sand
concrete t=50
plastic sheet
concrete t=50

Steel plate
t=7

▽ WL

60
75
40
311   351
351

426

▽ WL-426

Bridge bed
aluminum sheet
(white)
reinforced concrete
t=200
concrete t=50
plastic sheet
concrete t=50

50 50
200
300

▽ WL-726

Lighting

50   512   125 275

Chemical anchor
M12

Stainless base plate
t=12 w=400

AN 'ON-SITE' FACTORY This pavilion would perhaps have been impossible to build without the collaboration of a small construction firm, Aelbrecht Maes. At the first on-site meeting, only they among the several competitive builders had already produced a model of the honeycomb structure. We all found the abstract lines of honeycomb-and-patch pattern drawn in the air quite striking.

After that, several experimental models were made during the various design phases. As we made experimental models at the Tokyo studio, Aelbrecht Maes were experimenting with how to construct the pavilion, translating our scissors-and-glue paper renditions into machined and welded aluminum. We were in a different place, but we shared an 'on-site' feeling. Actually, the factory was very 'on-site' in this respect, because, in addition to the final design, 80% of the aluminum production and all the devices necessary for the execution were done at the factory in Bruges.

BRUGGE PAVILION. BRUGES, BELGIUM

Architects: Toyo Ito & Associates, Architects. Project member: Toyo Ito, Akihira Hirata, Hideyuki Nakayama. Structural Engineer: Structural Design Office Oak Inc. (Masato Araya). Coordination: Hera Van Sande, bdp Architects. Building area: 96.6m². Ceiling height: 3.36m. Maximum height: 3.61m. Client: Brugge 2002. Construction: Aelbrecht-Maes. Designing period: April 2000 – October 2001. Construction period: November 2001 – February 2002.

Masato Araya, engineer

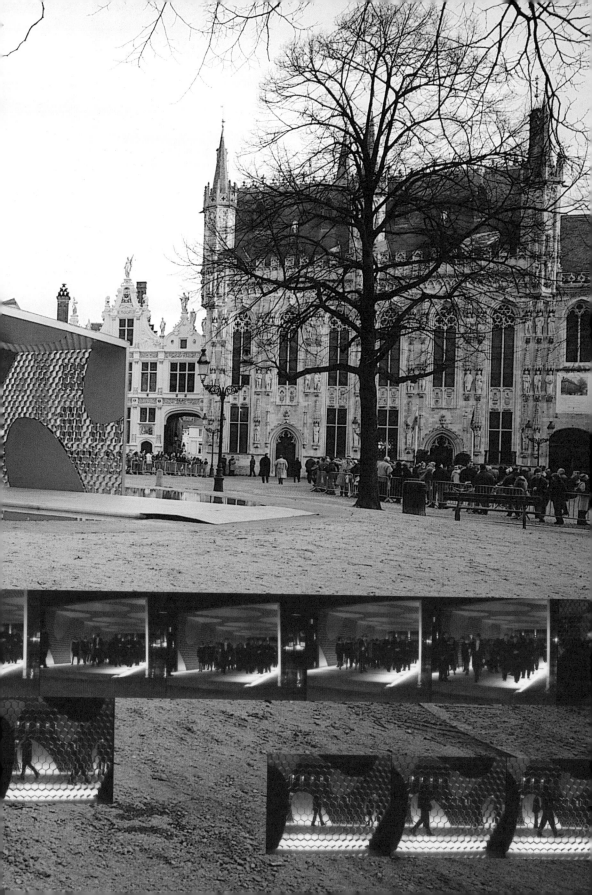

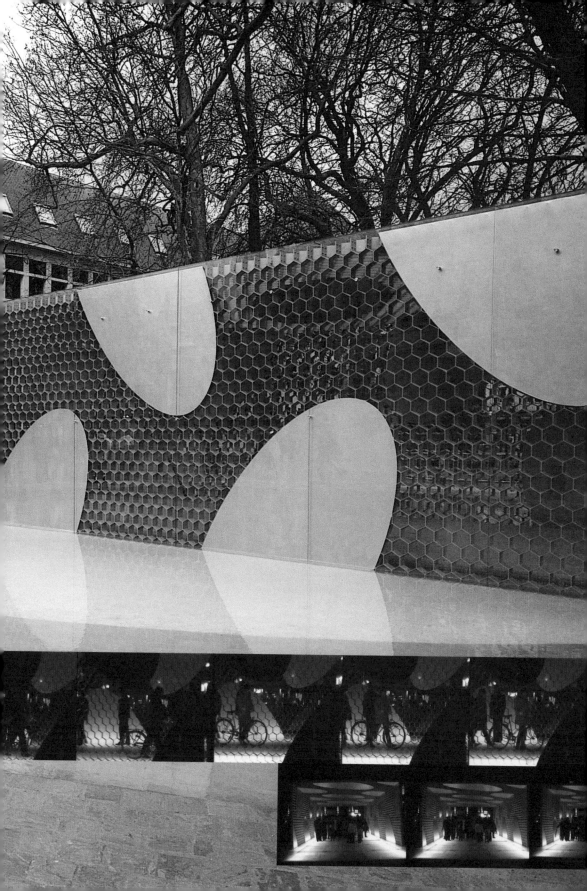

Kensington Gardens, London
Summer 2002

Serpentine Gallery Pavilion 2002 > Toyo Ito & Associates, Architects + Arup

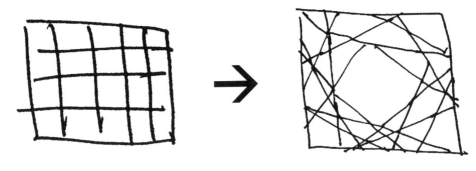

Usual grid beams

Serpentine Gallery rose beams

"Algorithm", Cecil Balmond > Usually to construct a rectangular or square roof, lines are drawn at right angles to each other, parallel to the sides of the plan, to produce a grid of beams. This roof plane is then supported by vertical columns placed evenly around the edges.

Instead of following the edges though, a more efficient pattern for the roof may be drawn by travelling across at an angle, say from half point on one side to the half point on the adjacent side. Repeating this for each side will produce an inner square wholly embedded within the first, but diagonal in orientation.

If the connection between adjacent sides is made more general, the start and end point of the first line may have different ratios. This puts a skew into the pattern, and once the new square is completed a virtual square is implied that goes beyond the boundaries of the original shape. Repeating the idea produces a spiral of shapes.

At the same time if all lines are projected forwards and backwards a dense field of crossed lines appear.

If anywhere on this two dimensional field the planes of a cube or box is laid out flat and then folded back again, the pattern picked up provides a continuous zigzag tracing over the three dimensional form.

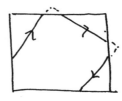

Instead of putting parallel beams, connect center points of each edge and repeat.
Move the imaginary junction out of the frame, shift the center, and extend all the lines.
Thus a regular pattern disappears.

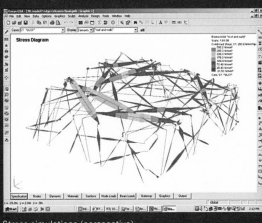

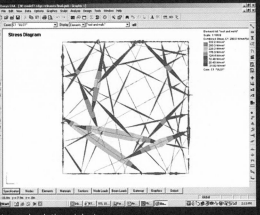

tress simulations (plan)

Stress simulations (perspective)

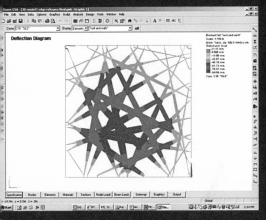

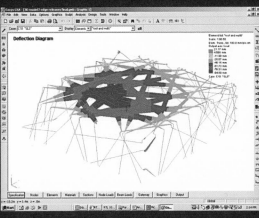

Deflection diagram (plan)

Deflection diagram (perspective)

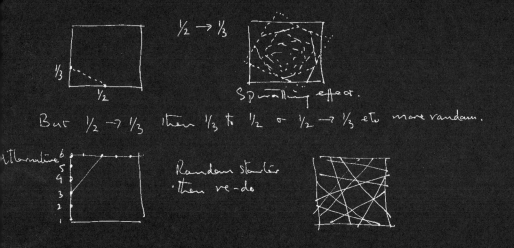

CONSTRUCTION A minimum size of steel flat is chosen to materialise all lines. Particular traces of the pattern are underlined and made thicker to act as structure. Normally the steel flat would be judged too weak to span much distance as beams, as the thin section buckles easily, but due to the side support made available from crossing elements in the pattern this particular weakness is easily overcome. The density offers a net of stability.

To aid construction on site the steel flats were welded together and assembled in zones – the algorithm identified triangular areas for panelising, as the squares rotated and reduced on the diagonal.

It is a surprise here how complexity has its own organisation and order, at one level scattered and distributed in a maze of mutual support, at another a set of zones whose margins are essential lines of structure. One interpretation is nested within the other.

The desire to categorise and keep things separate is challenged due to overlap – there is no beam or column in the conventional sense, no wall nor roof, 'in' is 'out' and vice versa. The pattern is open and keeps one guessing.

Like light, lines travel to all points, scattering rays to all corners, crossing over each other. What cannot be stopped is only intercepted. And the interruptions fold over, for a while, to make a pavilion on the summer lawn of the Serpentine.

Wall A, B, C & D
Phase 1

Panels 1A & 1B
Phase 2

Panels 2A & 2B
Phase 3

Panels 3A & 3B
Phase 4

Panels 4A, 4B, 4C & 4D
Phase 5

Panels 5A, 5B, 5C & 5D
Phase 6

Panels 6A, 6B & 6C
Phase 7

Panels 7
Phase 8

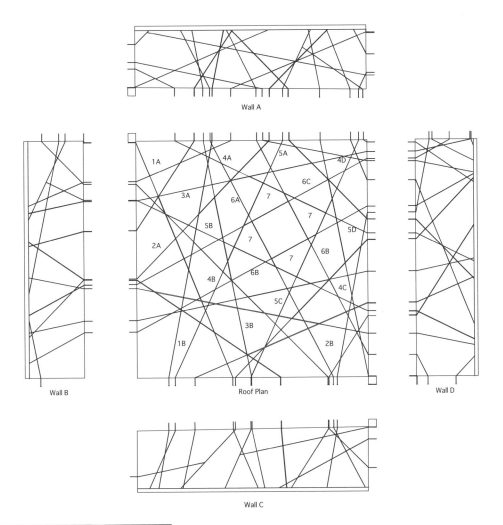

Wall A

Wall B

1A 4A 5A 4D
3A 6A 7 6C
5B 7
2A 5D
5C 7 6B
4B 6B 7
5C 4C
3B
1B 2B

Roof Plan

Wall D

Wall C

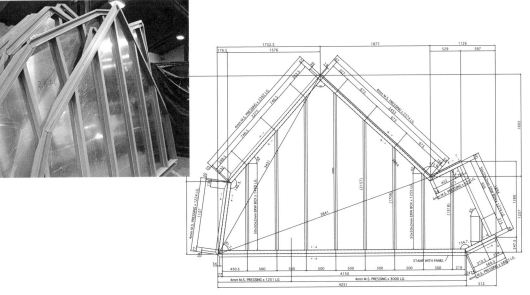

Panel detail

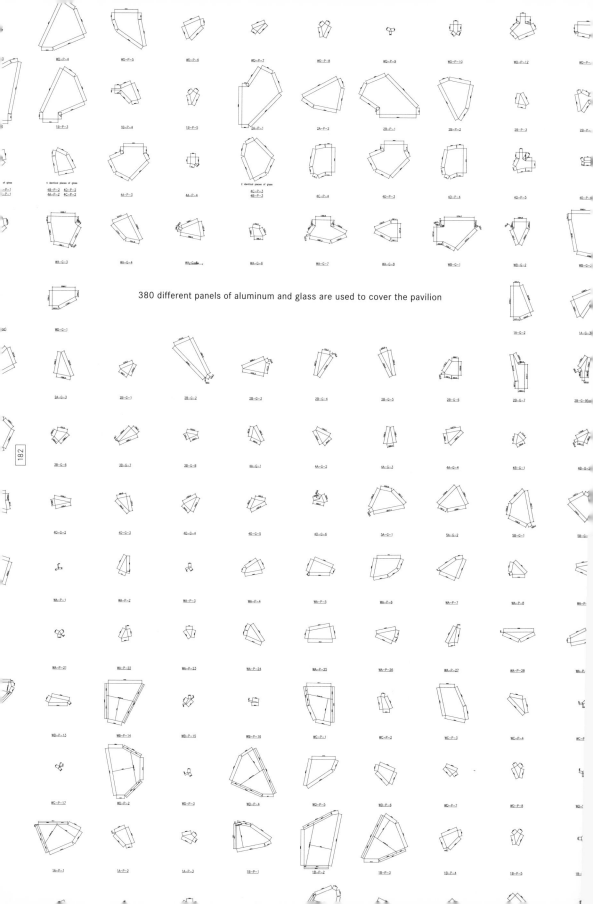

380 different panels of aluminum and glass are used to cover the pavilion

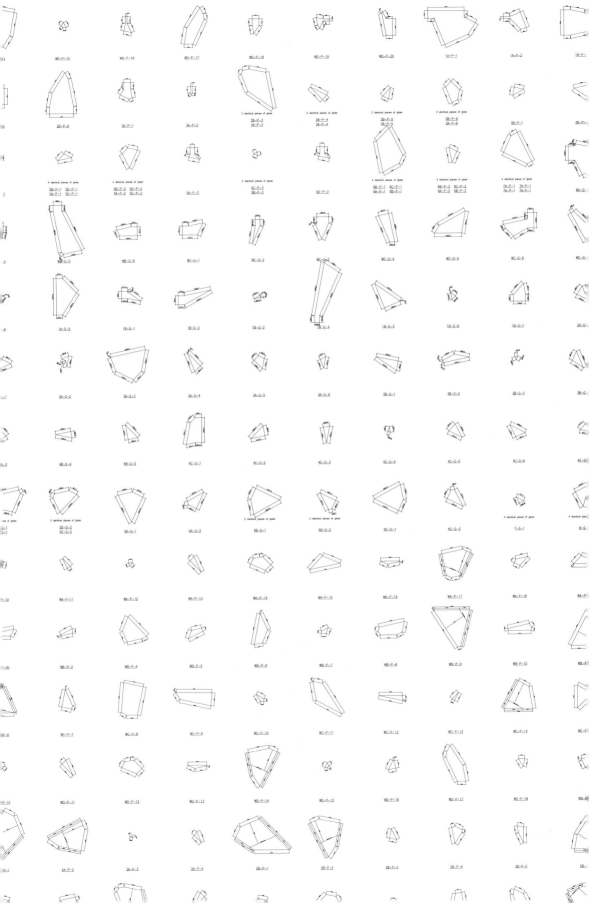

Glass panel setting

The center of the rose pattern

Aluminum panels and glass on the roof

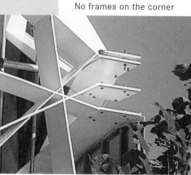

No frames on the corner

To not anchor the temporary pavilion to the ground, it has no foundation – the floor frame is just laid upon the greeen lawn.

Setting the steel members

SERPENTINE GALLERY PAVILION 2002. LONDON, UK

http://www.serpentinegallery.org

<u>Location:</u> Kensington Gardens, London, UK. <u>Architectural design:</u> Toyo Ito & Associates, Architects + Arup. <u>Architects:</u> Toyo Ito & Associates, Architects. <u>Project member:</u> Toyo Ito, Takeo Higashi, Hiromi Hosoya, Takayuki Miyoshi. <u>Structural design:</u> ARUP, Cecil Balmond (principal in charge), Charles Walker (project director) and Daniel Bosia (project engineer and algorithm), Pat Dallard (advisor on analysis), Chris Murgatroyd (materials and welding), Ray Ingles (CAD). <u>Client:</u> Serpentine Gallery. <u>Environment:</u> Arup. <u>Project management:</u> Mark Robinson and Julia Peyton-Jones, Serpentine Gallery. <u>Design term:</u> 01.2002 – 06.2002. <u>Construction term:</u> 04.2002 – 07.2002. <u>Completion date:</u> 07.2002. <u>Type of the site:</u> Public Park (Royal Park). <u>Building area:</u> 309.76 m². <u>Total floor area:</u> 309.76 m². <u>Maximum height:</u> 5.35m. <u>Main structure:</u> steel / steel grillage of flat bars.

Torrevieja
200 km south of Valencia

Relaxation Park in Torrevieja > Toyo Ito & Associates, Architects

This is a project for a "relaxation park" next to a salt lagoon, which is naturally pink in colour due the plankton it contains. It is known as a spa therapy resort, and surrounded by pre-fab housing for retired people, mostly from northern Europe. People come here for the curative salt mud baths. The city of Torrevieja wanted to develop this area as a spa for hydro/thalassotherapy, and requested Toyo Ito & Associates, Architects to design it.

The first step in this project was to create a landscape like a dune, with a univalve (sea snail) shell-shaped object containing three areas: a restaurant, information centre with changing and shower room, and open air bath. The structural design was developed with the collaboration of Masahiro Ikeda. Based upon the idea of reinforced concrete shells, the complete shell of spirals was obtained. In the design process, the form of the shell was softened with Bezier curves and turned into a semipermeable membrane held by osmotic pressure from inside and outside.

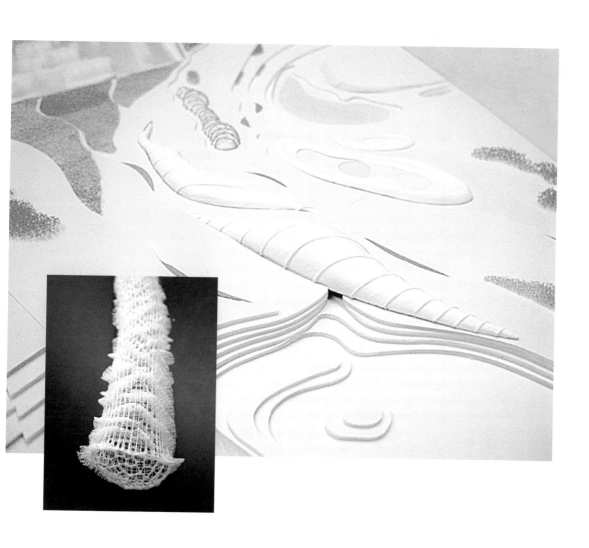

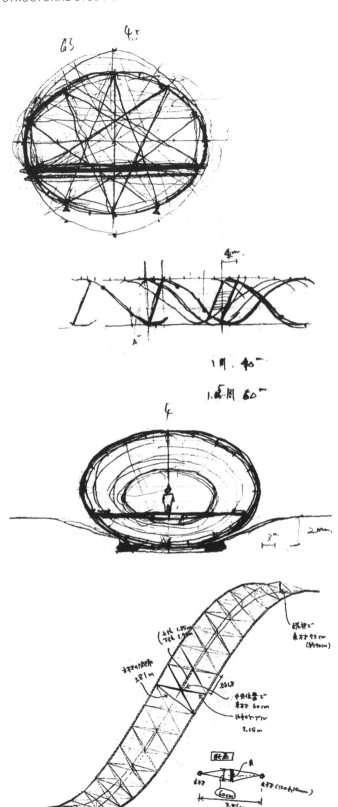

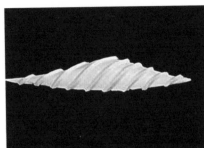

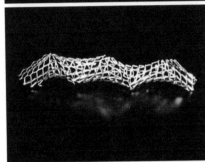

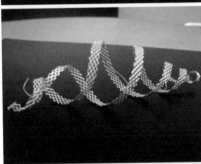

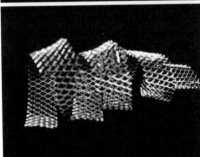

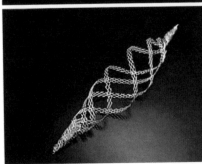

interior study model

interior study model

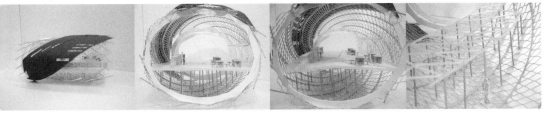

Truss structure model

Window study model

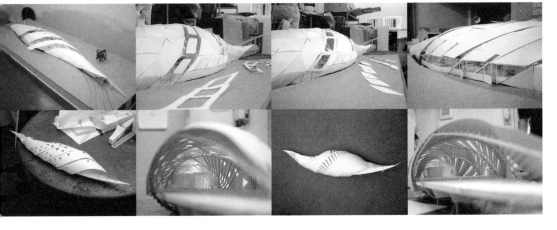

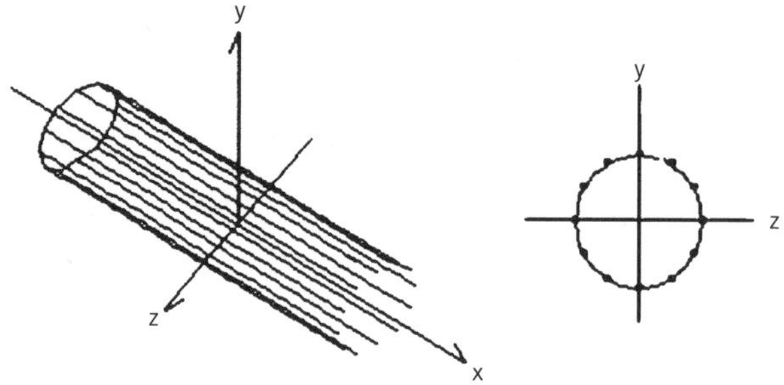

STRUCTURAL PROCESS

1. Make a straight tube
   (5m diameter)

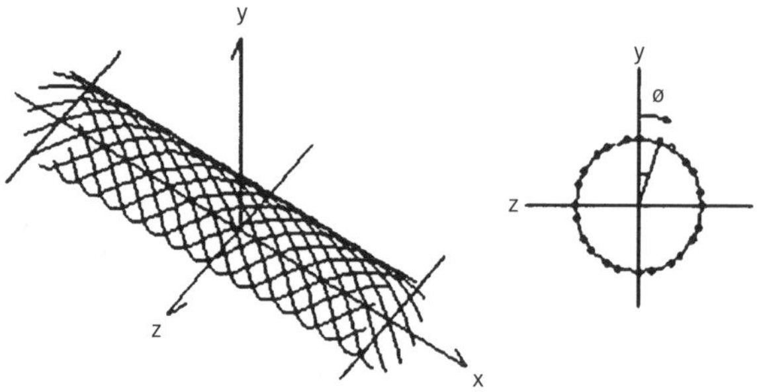

2. Twist it

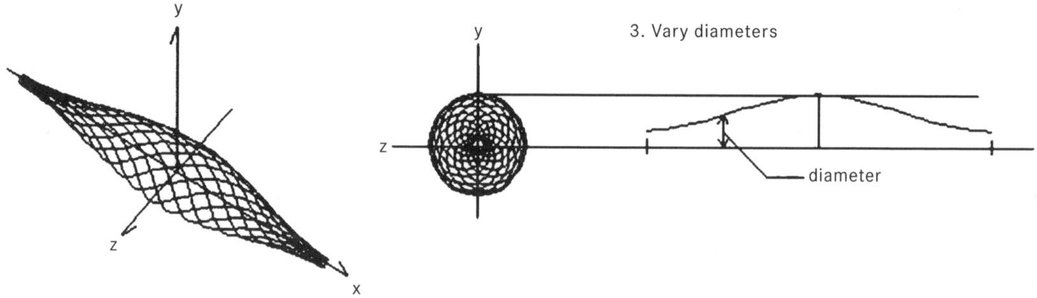

3. Vary diameters

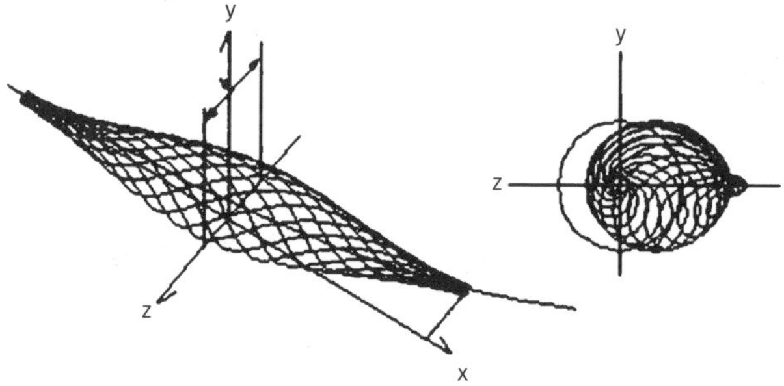

diameter

4. Curve the center line

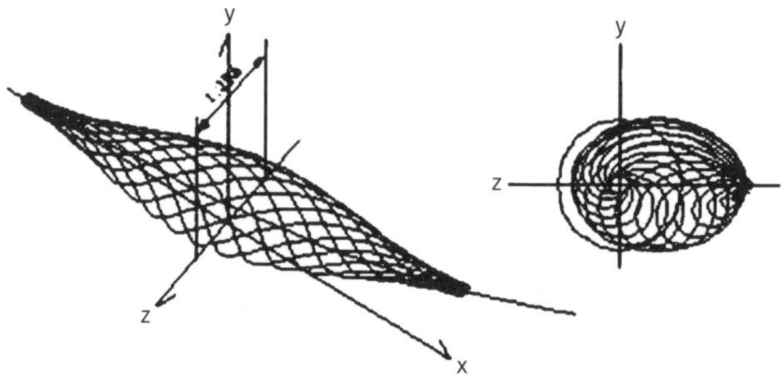

5. Widen in the Z-axis (x1.25)

Axonometric   Section

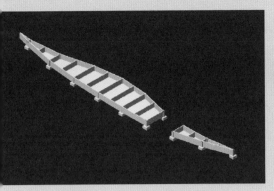

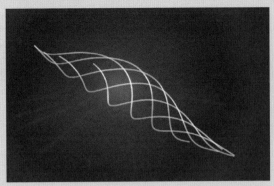

. BEZIER FOUNDATION
he foundation is made of concrete and divided
nto two areas. The outer line is continued from the
andscape with 2 bezier lines.

2A. SPIRAL SKIN
Spiral timber purlins form the surface of this shell and
5 spiral steel rods weave together to give the skin stability.
For construction, these steel rods can be erected first.

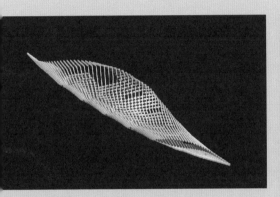

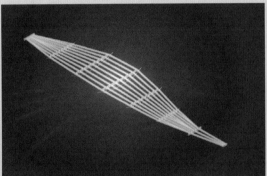

2B. SPIRAL SKIN
n some places, outside surfaces are covered by
imber plates so that all the material is integrated
and functions as one structural material.

3. HANGING FLOOR
Under gravity, we should think of mechanics as well as
mathematics and construction. The floor hangs from the
spiral skin and connects 5 spiral rods to each other to give
stability and strength to the spiral skin.

TIMBER PURLINS

6PAI/5 | 6PAI/5 | 6PAI/5
12PAI/5

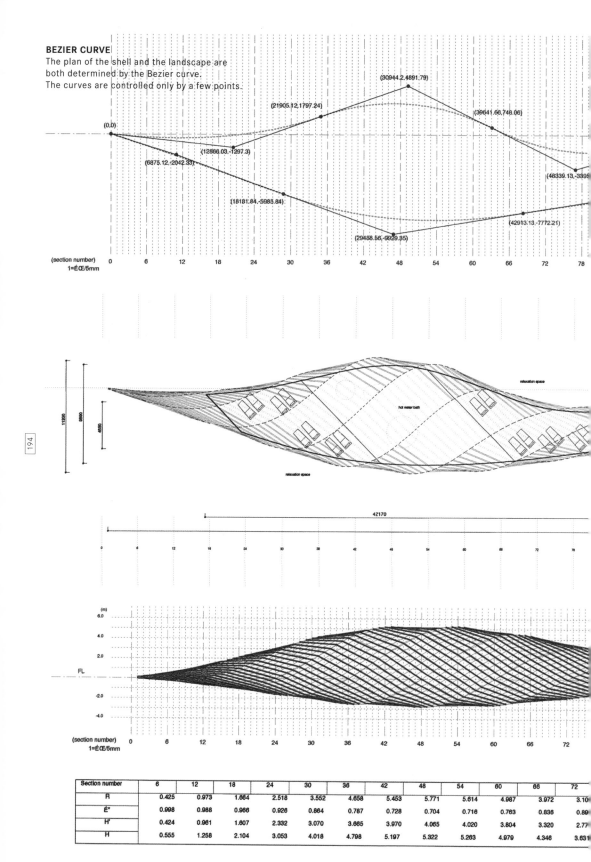

BEZIER CURVE
The plan of the shell and the landscape are
both determined by the Bezier curve.
The curves are controlled only by a few points.

(0,0)

(30944.2,4891.79)
(21905.12,1797.24)
(39641.66,748.06)
(12866.03,-1297.3)
(6875.12,-2042.33)
(48339.13,-3398)
(18181.84,-5985.84)
(42913.13,-7772.21)
(29488.56,-9929.35)

(section number) 0 6 12 18 24 30 36 42 48 54 60 66 72 78
1=ÉŒ/5mm

relaxation space
hot water bath
relaxation space

42170

0 6 12 18 24 30 36 42 48 54 60 66 72 78

(m)
6.0
4.0
2.0
FL
-2.0
-4.0

(section number) 0 6 12 18 24 30 36 42 48 54 60 66 72
1=ÉŒ/5mm

Section number	6	12	18	24	30	36	42	48	54	60	66	72
R	0.425	0.973	1.664	2.518	3.552	4.658	5.453	5.771	5.614	4.987	3.972	3.10
É"	0.998	0.988	0.966	0.926	0.864	0.787	0.728	0.704	0.716	0.763	0.836	0.89
H'	0.424	0.961	1.607	2.332	3.070	3.665	3.970	4.065	4.020	3.804	3.320	2.77
H	0.555	1.258	2.104	3.053	4.018	4.798	5.197	5.322	5.263	4.979	4.346	3.631

194

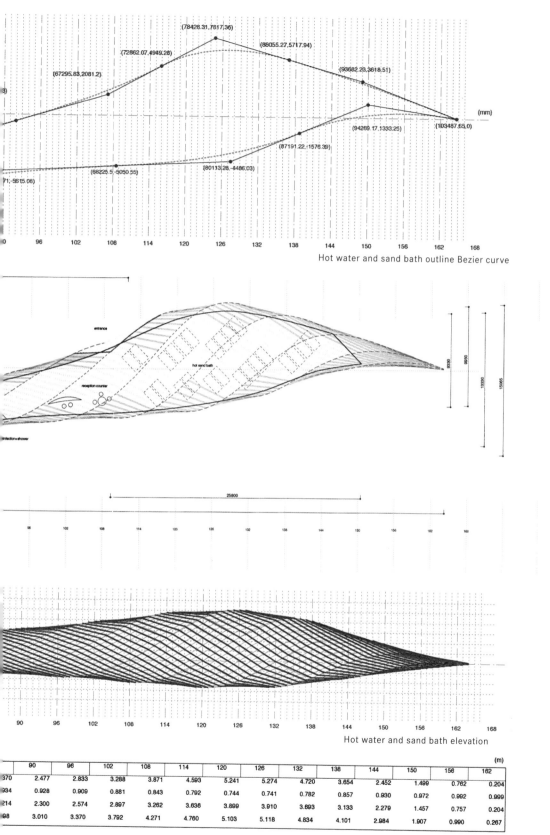

(78428.31,7817.36)

(86055.27,5717.94)

(72862.07,4949.28)

(67295.83,2081.2)

(93682.23,3618.51)

(94269.17,1333.25)

(103487.65,0)

(87191.22,-1576.39)

(68225.5,-5050.55)

(80113.28,-4486.03)

71,-5615.06)

(mm)

| 90 | 96 | 102 | 108 | 114 | 120 | 126 | 132 | 138 | 144 | 150 | 156 | 162 | 168 |

Hot water and sand bath outline Bezier curve

Hot water and sand bath elevation

Hot water and sand bath section data

	90	96	102	108	114	120	126	132	138	144	150	156	162
370	2.477	2.833	3.288	3.871	4.593	5.241	5.274	4.720	3.654	2.452	1.499	0.762	0.204
934	0.928	0.909	0.881	0.843	0.792	0.744	0.741	0.782	0.857	0.930	0.972	0.992	0.999
214	2.300	2.574	2.897	3.262	3.636	3.899	3.910	3.693	3.133	2.279	1.457	0.757	0.204
98	3.010	3.370	3.792	4.271	4.760	5.103	5.118	4.834	4.101	2.984	1.907	0.990	0.267

(m)

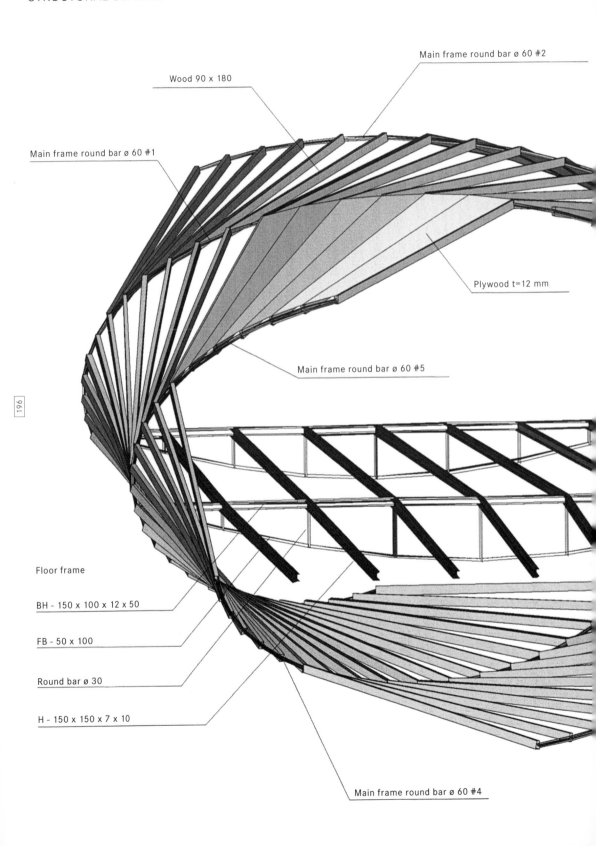

Main frame round bar ø 60 #2

Wood 90 x 180

Main frame round bar ø 60 #1

Plywood t=12 mm

Main frame round bar ø 60 #5

Floor frame

BH - 150 x 100 x 12 x 50

FB - 50 x 100

Round bar ø 30

H - 150 x 150 x 7 x 10

Main frame round bar ø 60 #4

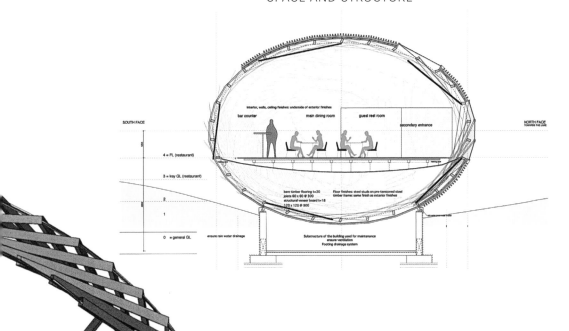

The basic structural system is a combination of a curved steel frame (five 60mm-diameter round bars), and a secondary timber frame (90 x 180) to connect the bars. The floors inside the shell are floating, and work structurally to keep the shell in tension and avoid flattening. The entire structure rests on an independent reinforced concrete foundation. 12mm-thick plywood sheets provide covering; wood was selected as the main material for the surface due to its appropriateness for the scale and functions of the facility and to shield the interior from sunlight and wind.

Main frame round bar ø 60 #3

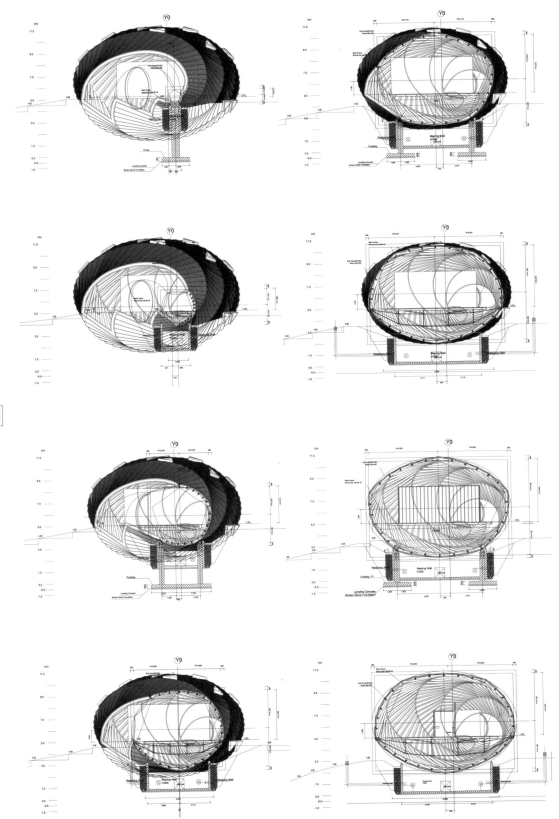

198

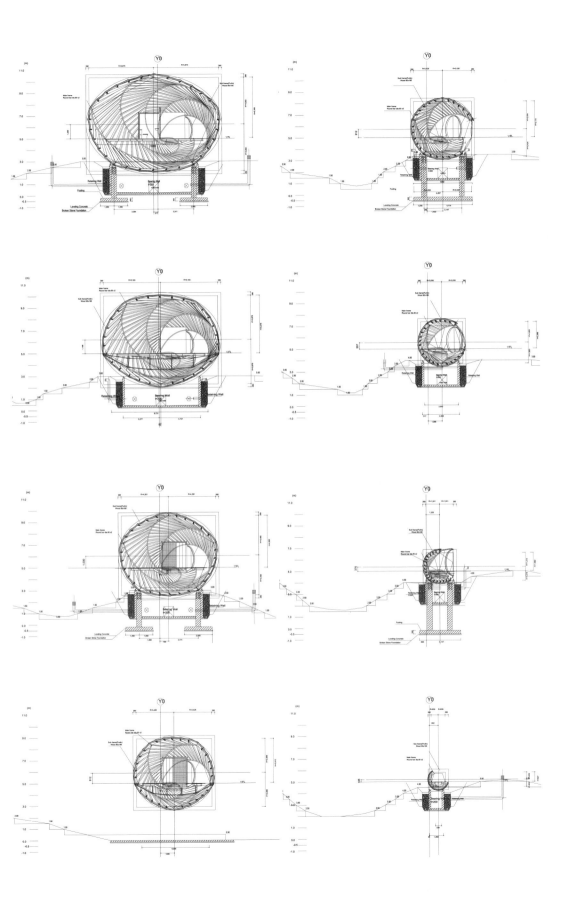

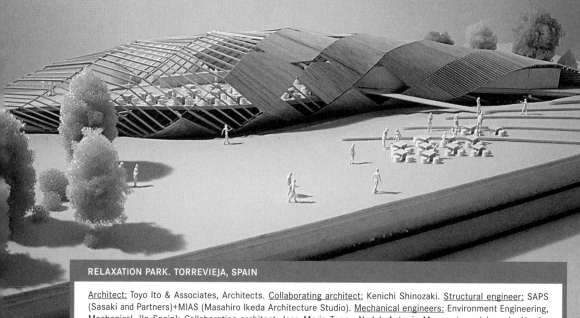

RELAXATION PARK. TORREVIEJA, SPAIN

Architect: Toyo Ito & Associates, Architects. Collaborating architect: Kenichi Shinozaki. Structural engineer: SAPS (Sasaki and Partners)+MIAS (Masahiro Ikeda Architecture Studio). Mechanical engineers: Environment Engineering, Mechanical. [In Spain]: Collaborating architect: Jose Maria Torres Nadal, Antonio Marquerie and Joaquin Alvado. Structural engineer: OMA (Obiol & Moya Arquitectes, S.C.P.). Location: Torrevieja, Spain. Building area: restaurant 275 m², dressing+shower room 345 m², open air bath 525 m². Client: The city Council of Torrevieja. Year of realization: end of 2004 (expected).

Omotesando Avenue, Tokyo

TOD'S OMOTESANDO SHOP. TOKYO, JAPAN

<u>Location:</u> Tokyo, Japan. <u>Function:</u> shop, office. <u>Site area:</u> 516.23 m². <u>Building area:</u> 401.51 m². <u>Total floor area:</u> 2,563.39 m². <u>Structure:</u> reinforced concrete, partially steel frame. <u>Number of stories:</u> 7 stories. <u>Completion:</u> Summer 2004. <u>Architect:</u> Toyo Ito & Associates, Architects (Toyo Ito, Takeo Higashi, Akihisa Hirata, Kaori Shikichi, Yasuaki Mizunuma). <u>Structure Engineer:</u> Structural Design Office Oak Inc. (Masato Araya). <u>Mechanical Engineer:</u> ES Associates Constructing Engineers. <u>Lighting:</u> Light Design.

In Toyo Ito's work, a specific material can grow and mutate across different projects over time. So the ordinary load-bearing column dissolves in the Mediatheque into a hollow tube that transmits not only structural forces but also people, information and light, then expands and changes orientation to become the horizontal envelope of the Torrevieja project. And from there to the box of the Brugge pavilion – really a flat tube with stiffening panels – where the web now turns into a honeycomb, integrating structure and opening in the same material; to the Serpentine pavilion, where the integration between structure and opening – solid and void – reaches a new level, and to Tod's, which synthesizes all of these developments.

Layering tree patterns creates random wall patterns as well as structure. This building is made with folding shadowgraph patterns.

Tod's Omotesando Building > Toyo Ito & Associates, Architects

Tod's is seven stories high, with a total floor area of 2,550m². The ground and first floors house Tod's retail boutique, the second, third and fourth floors are used as offices, the fifth floor as an event space, and the sixth floor contains a private dining room, meeting room and roof garden.

With its L-shaped plan, the building has six sides, and its most distinctive feature is these façades, which give the impression of a silhouetted row of zelkova trees. This complex pattern, generated by nine superimposed tree silhouettes, is expressed as a concrete structure with glass inserted into the openings. Window sashes are deliberately not used at the junctions of the concrete and glass in order to draw out the vitality and inherent qualities of the materials themselves through their direct physical juxtaposition. Compared with the other buildings that line Omotesando Avenue, most of which have standard glass façades, the advanced structural analyses and construction methods used to create this concrete grove will endow it with a unique and powerful presence.

The boutique on the first and second floors has an area of approximately 450m². The entrance, constructed from glass cut into crystal-like shapes, also serves as a display window. The natural light flowing into the building from every direction and the natural materials of the interior, such as wood and leather, combine to create a rich, beautiful space. Following the natural structure of a tree, the atmosphere of the upper levels differs from the lower boutique floors. The intersecting tree branches generate a relaxed ambiance for the office floors and the glamorous event space and roof garden. Gradually changing in character as it rises, the tree structure creates a series of attractive spaces.

Experience gained through many experimental projects – such as the Sendai Mediatheque, the Brugge 2002 Pavilion, and the Serpentine Pavilion in London – will bear fruit in the Tod's Omotesando Building. The construction is expected to take approximately one year.

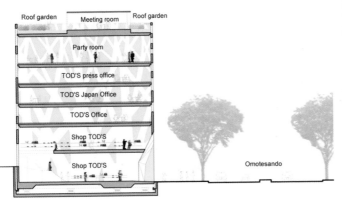

Roof garden   Meeting room   Roof garden

Party room

TOD'S press office

TOD'S Japan Office

TOD'S Office

Shop TOD'S

Shop TOD'S   Omotesando

Omotesando

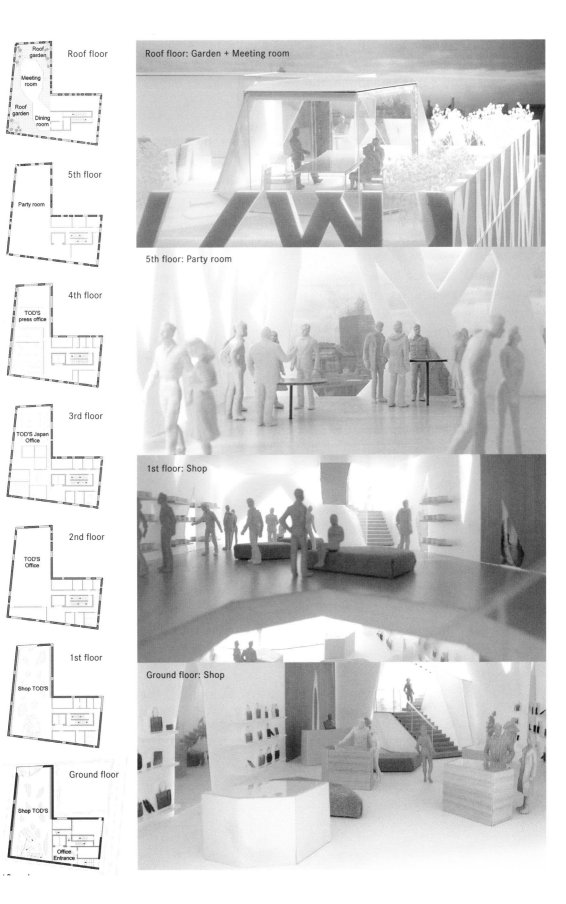

Roof floor

Roof garden
Meeting room
Roof garden
Dining room

5th floor

Party room

4th floor

TOD'S press office

3rd floor

TOD'S Japan Office

2nd floor

TOD'S Office

1st floor

Shop TOD'S

Ground floor

Shop TOD'S

Office Entrance

Roof floor: Garden + Meeting room

5th floor: Party room

1st floor: Shop

Ground floor: Shop

Building Intelligence

Neil Gershenfeld (Director) and Raffi Krikorian (Graduate student)
MIT Media Lab, Center for Bits and Atoms
http.//cba.mit.edu/
www.media.mit.edu

ARCHITECTURE

MIT's Media Laboratory is embarking on an ambitious construction project that will significantly enlarge its intellectual as well as its physical space. Along with rebuilding its existing I.M. Pei building, the Pritzker-Prize-winning architect Fumihiko Maki has designed an adjoining new 59,741 m² building. Site preparation for this structure began in the fall of 2001, with construction starting in 2002 and occupancy expected early in 2005.

Along with existing Media Lab activities, this facility will house new initiatives including the Center for Bits and Atoms, which will bring together both the technical and theoretical infrastructure required to simultaneously shape the content of information and its physical properties at scales from atomic nuclei to global networks, and the Okawa Center for Future Children, which will be exploring internally and externally the impact of emerging information technologies on the development of children and the environments they live in around the globe.

These resources are all being designed in the Media Lab tradition of large interdisciplinary shared workspaces. The building is divided into interlocking multi-story labs built around a soaring central atrium with transparent elevators, to enhance the visibility within and among the labs. For maximum flexibility, building services are distributed and accessed via a re-configurable floor system that provides distributed access to data and power on a 4-foot grid throughout the lab and office spaces. Walls serve only to provide visual and aural isolation where needed and can easily be relocated.

This flexible arrangement will necessarily create unusual adjacencies, such as bringing small children near dangerous machine tools. In such an environment it is essential that the building be able to accommodate and respond to the changing needs of both its occupants and the physical plant itself. For this reason, the building is also being designed as a testbed for fine-grained Internet connectivity in the infrastructure, along with scalable distributed computing to operate it. This document explains what is being done, why, and how, with a focus on the role of using low data-rate IP protocols over mature RS485 and powerline wiring to low-cost powered devices. It will serve as an active tracking site throughout the life of the project.

VISION

The logical architecture of the building rests on two key beliefs: first, that Internet connectivity must be extended to the most rudimentary components of the building, rather than mediated through intermediate devices. Second, that each of these elements must contain enough data and processing power to be able to execute and locally reprogram its functions without assuming the existence of another computer. These are both driven by concern for scalability. While the desirability of Internet connectivity is perhaps obvious, its necessity warrants comment. There are many other standards in use for home and industrial networking, including X10, Lonworks, CAN bus, emWare, BACnet, and CCN. While all of these have merits in the domains for which they were developed, all face some combination of the same scaling problems that the suite of Internet protocols (IP, UDP, TCP, ARP, etc.) address: limited interoperability, restrictive embedded assumptions about how they will be used, lack of discovery and routing through hierarchical networks, limited addressing, and proprietary licensing restrictions.

Fixing these problems will bring each of these alternatives closer to both the technical and social architecture of the Internet, suggesting that it would be better to jump to using the Internet protocols directly. The primary historical reason why this has not been done has been their cost, measured in dollars as well as relevant resources such as milliWatts, package pins, or installation effort. But work at the Media Lab and elsewhere has shown that a complete Internet node can be implemented with a few hundred bytes of code, corresponding to a few thousand transistors, or tens of cents worth of silicon. What makes this possible is "delayering": most of the code and complexity in the Internet stack in a conventional computer is associated with inter-layer message passing, which is a technical reflection of the human bureaucracies that develop and use them. A dedicated stack in a device as simple as a light switch can reduce this overhead by orders of magnitude while still remaining standards-compliant.

Another reason why there are so many competing standards is the differences in their performance requirements. While it is possible to run the Internet protocols over physical layers that provide guarantees on bandwidth and latency, the typical timing of commodity networks can exceed the time scale of many "real-time" requirements by so many orders of magnitude that a probabilistic performance bound does provide a statistically significant system guarantee. For example, from the 10-msec time scale of human perception to the 10-nsec time scale of an ethernet bit, there are 6 orders of magnitude available for protocol overhead.

A more severe but less obvious issue with using Internet protocols is their hidden cost. When a permanent computer is added to a network in a building, a system operator must assign it a network address, associate that address with both a name and a media access address, register that name at a name server, make sure that the computer is properly configured to find names and routes, and provide services the computer might need including file storage, backups, and remote software maintenance.

The fractional cost of the sysop's time and servers dedicated to the new computer is acceptable if the computer costs $1,000, but not if it costs $1. If a light bulb or elevator call button is to be economically connected to the

Internet, it can't be assumed that a support person will be responsible for its configuration.

An alternative is suggested by the simple X10 home automation protocol, which uses a small set of addresses to enable devices such as lights and switches to directly communicate. This notion can be generalized to an embedded IP device by giving it a simple data structure that contains addresses of devices that it needs to communicate with, along with fragments of algorithms specifying the conditions under which messages are sent between them, and the conditions under which these data can be changed. Many such devices taken together then form a giant distributed data structure, as well as a distributed parallel computer that processes relevant information. Rather than necessarily routing messages through servers, as is now done in many building control systems, the servers become descriptive rather than prescriptive: they can observe and interact with the network nodes, but are not necessary to operate them.

If local devices do not rely on remote computers, then it must be possible to program them locally. This requires a locally-accessible notion of identity. To connect to the Internet a computer must have a numerical address (e.g., 18.85.0.1), and it can have an easier-to-remember name (e.g., media.mit.edu). Both of these intentionally have no spatial meaning, and hence don't capture a local sense of identity (e.g., "the switch on the wall next to my office door"). For this reason, an essential element of the system design will be the role of local interactions in determining functional identity. A light switch could be introduced to a light that it is to control by, for example, pushing a programming button on the switch followed by one on the light, or using a wired or wireless tool to carry the address from one to the other. In either case, the user introduces an association by physical interaction, then the devices communicate over the network to update their data structures and control algorithms. Such physical interactions can easily be extended to represent one-to-many and many-to-one controls, as well as analog decisions. All of these could still be set remotely over the network, but-crucially-they don't need to be.

There are many consequences of such an architecture. It is more reliable, because the single points of failure in the servers have been eliminated (a vulnerability that has been brought home by the dramatic failure of some building control systems following damage to the building). And it is cheaper to build, because just two such devices form a useful system rather than requiring central services. Even more importantly, it is cheaper to build because the logical configuration does not need to be reduced in advance to a detailed specification. Instead of preparing drawings showing how lights will connect to switches, and having a contractor (hopefully) follow those drawings during construction, it is necessary only to provide connections to power and data for the lights and switches and then their associations can be established later by the users. These savings recur if the use of the space changes, requiring change in the control associations.

Perhaps even more significant is the economic impact of operating such a building. An obvious application is energy efficiency. For example, the air supplied to a room can be locally adjusted based not just on a thermostat setting, but also on aggregating data including the number of people in the room and the state of the windows and outside air. The room's variable air volume (VAV) unit can receive information directly from those devices and act appropriately. That in turn leads to an even greater prospective impact: on human efficiency. The people in a building usually cost much more than the energy used by the building. If, in the same example, the data fusion and computation distributed over the sensors can help a room determine not just it temperature but the comfort of its occupants, the impact on their productivity could be much more dramatic than just a reduction in energy consumption.

Finally, the most intriguing aspect of a programmable building lies in the intersection of its logical and physical architecture. Right now there is a clear division of labor, with one architect determining the character of the physical space, and another the organization of its network and computing. But as these components become more tightly integrated, so will their functions. Inevitably, this will lead to a richer notion of "architect", as the designer of the space can also shape the look and feel of active aspects including lighting and modes of interaction, while the work of the designer of the network can be seen in physical as well as digital worlds.

In the Media Lab, an early seed of this activity was the work of a precocious undergrad, Matt Hancher. In 1999 he started development of the "Filament" series of circuit boards, building on the work of Pehr Anderson and Rob Poor. These paired a simple microcontroller with an ethernet controller and twisted-pair media access in order to effectively provide a serial port with an IP address using just tens of dollars in parts. In its first incarnation it simply turned ASCII bytes into broadcast UDP packets.

This was developed for practical reasons, because a number of Lab projects growing out of activities associated with the Things That Think Consortium were building devices and interfaces outside of traditional computers, and they needed a way to communicate without tying them to a conventional computer. An example is an installation at the Museum of Modern Art in New York in 1999 that sought to provide supporting electronic information for a landmark architecture exhibition (The Un-Private House) by using the furniture in the gallery as an information interface, rather than by imposing kiosks that would take visitors out of the visual and social space of the museum. A telling comment came at the opening, when a beaming elderly Trustee of the museum expressed her delight with the installation by proclaiming that she hates computers, but that here she could access information without using a computer. What made it possible were 17 Filaments in a table, along with many other embedded microcontrollers, but in a very real sense having so much computing so finely distributed does effectively make it disappear as a distinguishable entity.

The next important step came with the arrival of H. Shrikumar, who is notable for having squeezed a complete Web server into a few hundred bytes of code and fit it into an 8-bit 8-pin processor that costs about a dollar in commodity quantities. This suggested that low-cost nodes such as the Filament could be viewed both as servers and as clients, providing information in a form that is directly accessible to any Web browser. But Shri's work also underscored the hidden cost in machines and people if such Web nodes relied on information in conventional servers in order to be able to carry out their commands, which led to his development of distributed data structures and control algorithms so that the information associated with a device could be resident in the device. Then, inspired by the ideas of Prof. Hiroshi Ishii, a tangible interface was provided so that physical interactions could update these data.

Design development of the Media Lab's expansion began in 2000, and the next major project milestone came in August 2001 in a jointly-developed trial with United Technologies showing Carrier Comfort Network (CCN) devices such as fan coils and thermostats interfaced to embedded Web servers with both local and remote readout and programming. This was followed by a test installation in Barcelona in September 2001, developed with the Metapolis architectural collective led by Vicente Guallart and Enric Ruiz and supported by a network of Catalan institutions. This group sought to pick up where Antoni Gaudí left off. Gaudí brought enormous expressiveness to structural engineering, showing how it could be essential to an architect's creative communication. But not only has that tight integration receded with the rise of engineering through independent subcontracting teams, the increasingly important computational architecture of a building is nearly universally a completely independent subsystem overlaid onto it.

Working with the Metapolis and Catalan teams, this project developed a structural system based around channels from Eutrac, so that each beam guided structural forces, AC power, DC power, and data. These were used to construct a test house in a theatrical space, with the tiny network nodes shown against a backdrop of what might be the world's largest Web browser. This installation demonstrated on a much larger scale how the elements of embedded IP and distributed control with tangible interfaces could operate, and in fact was particularly validated because much of the effort in debugging the installation lay with the instabilities of conventional computer operating systems rather than the relative predictability of the embedded nodes.

The installation team included leaders in the "Internet 2" effort that is developing ultra-high-speed network technology. By the end of the project, the track system was referred to as "Internet 0," because it sought to create a layer below today's Internet that provides a foundation for its interface to the physical world, and because of the shared belief that significant new value in future network growth will lie in low-bit-rate embedded applications in areas such as health care. These ideas will be further explored with MIT's Home of the Future effort.

The planned building construction schedule was for contracts to be awarded over the summer of 2002, followed by the start of construction, then for major control components (such as air handlers) to be installed in 2003, distributed devices (such as thermostats) in 2004, and occupancy in 2005.

Following opening, the building is expected to serve as both a showcase for the new products installed and as a testbed for exploring higher-value aspects of building intelligence beyond its basic functionality, such as predictive modeling of user needs, and feedback control based on more sophisticated measures of the comfort and efficiency of the occupants. And as the products mature they are likely to be used in follow-up flagship structures on a commercial basis with partners, such as a Frank Gehry commission back in Barcelona.

IMPLEMENTATION

The architecture of the most complete installation to date, in Barcelona, sought to use existing standards as much as possible, but necessarily entailed some new development at their interfaces. The physical transport chosen for the data in the track system was RS485, because of its ubiquity in building control systems, and more importantly because its electrical interface permits the network geometry to be arbitrary. This is essential because the structure could have multiple branches and closed loops in the mechanical design, which would necessarily be reflected in the electrical layout, and any of the communication alternatives that require impedance matching at junctions would impose active hubs at mechanical connections, significantly adding to the construction complexity as well as cost. A passive multidrop network was taken as an essential design constraint.

The decision to use topology-independent RS485 limited the bit rate in the track to on the order of 100 kbps, so that reflections from discontinuities in a building-scale structure could be ignored over the time scale of a bit. While this is very slow compared to current networks, the target applications are low-bit-rate devices, and the desirability of the ease of installation became rapidly evident during construction. The use of RS485 provided reliable communications with a dollar-scale cost of physical media access circuitry as well as compatibility with the enormous industrial installed base of RS485 systems. In most installations (like Barcelona, and the Media Lab's new building) it is likely to coexist with a wireless 802.11 network. 802.11 provides 10 Mbps, along with mobility, but comes at a much higher per-node cost, along with a need for an independent power source. The RS485/IP system was aimed at simple relatively-fixed components such as lights and switches; 802.11 is appropriate for more expensive mobile devices such as laptops and PDAs. 802.11 could of course be used to provide a higher-bandwidth channel to more expensive devices that use the track for power and mechanical assembly as well as local I/O.

Beyond providing a mechanical mounting for devices, two rails in the track were used to supply an AC hot and neutral, two rails were used for 9V DC and ground, and two were used for the differential RS485 signaling. The AC served to power appliances such as lamps. While it was not necessary to separately provide DC, this reduced the complexity of the network nodes since they would otherwise all need DC power supplies. The differential data encoding provided good noise immunity; the runs could easily be larger than the natural logical scale of a segment.

RS485 imposes no constraints on the logical signaling used over the physical layer; we used a conventional UART to encode with serial ASCII framing the bytes of IP packets, along with their UDP or TCP headers. These were compressed from 40 to 6 bytes to save bandwidth by removing unnecessary fields, just as headers are compressed in a PPP modem connection. Although interoperability was not an issue because there are no legacy IP-over-RS485 devices to talk to, such compression is easily removed for a standard SLIP encoding. For the Barcelona installation dedicated messages were defined to represent the kinds of nodes and their messages, but the packet payload could easily carry either proprietary protocols such as Carrier Comfort Network being tunneled through an IP transport, or open-standard messages such as XML.

A number of IP-enabled devices were developed to interface to the RS485 network, including buttons, digital and analog I/O interfaces, a triac module for AC switching, and a serial port targeted at communicating with a reader of low-cost ID tags, and an ethernet interface to connect to a conventional

CAT5-wired network. Beyond providing connectivity to remote networks, the ethernet interface is also important for scalability. RS485 has limits in both the bandwidth and fanout of a single segment (32-128 devices, depending on interface input impedance), and hence is appropriate for directly connecting logically-related devices, such as a lighting track or a room control system. These segments can then be joined with ethernet connections to active hubs, which is an acceptable cost at the segment level.

The Barcelona project used RS485 for the physical layer, for both its convenience in a new installation and its compatibility with existing building control components, but a powerline version of this system will be developed for use with existing wiring. Emerging standards such as HomePlug use aggressive modulation schemes to attain reasonable data rates over noisy and lossy powerlines, bringing the cost above the leaf nodes targeted here, but by dropping the data rate to the speeds required by control systems it becomes possible to use much simpler software RF techniques to provide reliable modulation for the shared-channel serial protocols. And although the Barcelona installation did not use wireless nodes because the focus was on the building rather than user mobility, they will be developed for mobile nodes. Below the cost and bit rate of 802.11, possible wireless protocols include both IRDA and Bluetooth. Neither of these was designed for native peer-to-peer IP traffic, but both can carry such messages as payloads. Emerging research transports will also be investigated.

IP-enabling a building does raise a range of security concerns, as well as pointing to possible solutions. Restricting remote access to approved uses and users will require reliable network security, but that is no different from the demands placed on any corporate firewall that protects sensitive information, and the device implementations can use cryptographic standards such as IPSEC and SSH. Added security can be provided by associating logical access with physical access, so that potentially dangerous operations require authentication by a device in person as well as over the network, and vulnerable parts of the network are kept separate from ones that are intentionally easily accessible. There is also a risk of physical damage caused by incorrect commands accidentally executed by authorized users; this will

require clearly identifying in the protocol implementation the fixed functionality
required by the manufacturer, and the circumstances under which users can
add associations onto it.

STANDARDIZATION
Although IP is a mature open standard, embedding it in building systems raises
a number of standards questions. This starts with the form factor. The track
system used for the Barcelona installation was convenient where mechanical
access needed to be distributed, and could be standardized as conventional
lighting tracks have been. But for distributed control systems there will need
to be a standard for separate electrical connectors and wiring. And if the
integration with structural systems is further developed, there will need to be a
standard for their form factors and joining systems.
RS485 does not specify how channel contention is handled, which is not an
issue in a conventional master-slave configuration, but it does need to be addressed for peer-to-peer networking. Both here and for low data-rate powerline
signaling, activity detection as well as modulation will need to be specified as
part of the media access to implement CSMA/CD-like channel sharing.
At the logical layer, either a dedicated IP port could be defined for these
messages, or an existing port such as 80 (for HTTP packets) could be used. HTTP
does add overhead, but also provides immediate interoperability. The obvious
way to standardize the messages sent over HTTP would be through an XML
definition, such as those in Universal Plug and Play or Brazil.
The node addressing could use IPV4, which is widely deployed, but the 32 bits of
address space would require that the local segments do some kind of Network
Address Translation internally in order to reuse addresses. IPV6 provides 128
bits for addressing (corresponding to roughly 1000 addresses per square meter
over the Earth's surface). That's easily enough to assign a unique address to any
device, but isn't yet compatible with all Internet-connected computers.
These questions span the levels of description of many standard bodies,
including IETF, IEEE, ISO, ANSI, EIA, and DIN. An open meta-standardization
question is the appropriate home for these issues. This is not something that
this project can answer directly, but it can contribute by providing exemplary

embodiments of complete systems, as well as helping identify the fundamental guiding principles, and then deferring to the community of partners on the implementation details.

SPONSORSHIP
Corporate partners are working with this project at many levels. At the highest, a number of companies have made naming grants for spaces in the new building, in order to seed long-term activity in areas of joint interest, and develop strategic partnerships to jointly manage relevant resources for shared activities on both sides. These include Motorola for embedded processing, Lego for play, MasterCard for financial transactions, Swatch for design, and British Telecom and Telmex for communications. Corporate Research Partners are members across the Media Labs and base a research group there; these also include companies such as HP, Intel, the United States Postal Service, and eircom. Sponsors of Media Lab research consortia and of the Center for Bits and Atoms receive royalty-free rights to all of the shared intellectual property; this cost tracks the carrying cost of a research employee, and buys the work of about 400 people in a $40M/yr program. Below that, affiliate sponsors participate in the programs without free intellectual property access, and a number of vendors are providing materials at internal costs as part of their participation in the project.
Along with free access to intellectual property, the Labs work closely with the sponsors on developing and transferring reductions to practice so that their much-more-expensive internal labor can start with things that are known to work, and the Labs also help provide a context for this effort, including external visibility and partnerships across the sponsor community. Over the lifecycle of the building project, research prototypes will be introduced into sponsor products, debugged and installed in the building as a launch test site, then used for both market visibility and the development of added-value services.

MIT, Cambridge, 2000

Sergi Jordà

Artur Serra

Neil Gershenfeld

Vicente Guallart

Enric Ruiz-Geli

Media House Project > IAAC Metapolis + MIT Media Lab +
Fundació Politècnica de Catalunya + I2Cat + Elisava

Directed by Vicente Guallart, Enric Ruiz-Geli, Willy Müller (Matapolis), Neil Gershenfeld (MIT Media Lab),
Pau Roig (Fundació Politècnica de Catalunya), Artur Serra (I2Cat) and Núria Díaz (Elisava)

The IAAC (Institut d'Arquitectura Avançada de Catalunya) grew out of the Metapolis
Institute of Advanced Architecture, and is conceived as an exchange of energies:
a nodal point in a network linking the leading international study centres currently
engaging in research on the interface between the construction of the virtual world
and the construction of the physical world. The IAAC is envisaged as a place for the
investigation, production and diffusion of ideas in diverse environments, a place for
the hybridization of knowledge and interaction with other disciplines, drawing on
the diversity of potentials that come together in Barcelona: city, university, industry
and creation, research, development, (e)ducation and diffusion (R+3D). In order to
make this possible, the next few years will see the launch of a series of activities, as
consortia are set up with the various institutions and firms that will have a hand in
developing this communal space.

Vicente Guallart > The "Media House Project" is conceived as a strategic alliance,
the purpose of which is to combine the respective potentialities of the MIT's Media
Lab and its technological environment, oriented primarily towards the enabling
technology, and of Metapolis Institute for Advanced Architecture in Barcelona (now
the IAAC - Institut d'Arquitectura Avançada de Catalunya) and its creative and artistic
environment, oriented towards the design of the public and the private space, with
the goal of putting forward proposals for the development of a new interaction
between the physical world and the digital world, in order to lay the foundations of a
new "art of dwelling".
Every age has produced a particular way of dwelling as a reflection of its specific
conditions – social, economic and cultural – and technological developments: the
piping of water into the home led to the appearance of the kitchen and the bathroom;
artificial light and electricity resulted in new forms of organization in the home;
domestic appliances allowed people to conserve food for longer periods and to do
more in less time, and TV turned the traditional living room into a window on a world

dominated by the mass media. In our own time, the new technologies of information and communications are transforming the home into a micro-city, a genuinely multifunctional environment (work, shopping, leisure, rest) from which to inhabit the global village.

Within a few years the passive physical world defined by purely functional structures which give people shelter, and in which we consume products and interact with the world by way of screens, will be rendered obsolete by intelligent environments in which everyone and everything (people, objects, spaces) will both generate and consume information and (ideally) transform it into knowledge.

Architecture, which organizes human activity by means of the construction of space, has the potential to play a key role in this new situation if we can transform it into the best interface for interacting in the new hybrid situation we will find ourselves inhabiting.

This being so, the design of both physical space and digital space are going to have to take place at the same time, in a process of constant feedback in which both worlds learn from their own and each other's potentialities and limitations. Matter and information will intersect in activities.

The knowledge society will develop a home geared towards knowledge, a place primed for the creation and representation of knowledge, in which the individual, the citizen, in relation with other citizens around the world, can live a life of quality. This project promotes the creation of environments that are less technologically cluttered, more beautiful, more meaningful, that help people shape their environment and connect to others.

The "Media House" will not be "a house with a computer"; instead, the house will be the computer. As Neil Gershenfeld says, architecture will never be inert again.

Manuel Gausa, Theoretical framework > 'Things that think' – a term coined by the Media Lab – operate in reactive environments: houses, buildings and public spaces sensitive to the incidence of information and its development in mechanisms within and with which they relate and interact with one another. The innovation with which the digital world is constructed needs to be carried over into the physical world.

Technological advances in effect make it possible – and with ever increasing rapidity – not only to simulate models of growth but to animate structures, anticipate processes and generate flexible, interactive systems whose definition is based on fundamental patterns/programmes and duly processed and transformed messages/data. The digital world is ushering in – it is still in its early stages – a space rich in embryonic possibilities; a space open to new programmes and new spatial definitions born of operative environments/systems ("reactive" mechanisms) that are capable of "reacting" to and "mutating" with reality, and thus capable of "tuning in" to and "acting" in and with it at the same time. This heralds a new period of architecture in relation with other spheres of production, a new phase that will in all probability see the introduction of previously unimagined – or at best vaguely intuited – techniques and formal concepts in every aspect of the construction – and the whole conception, representation, design and simulation – of a dynamic and changing, evolving and elastic space and its connection with the very development of techniques and technologies themselves. These dynamics affirm themselves as merely the "potential" of what is anticipated as a new "phase" among the last vestiges and reformulations of modernity, the most forceful manifestations of which can be envisaged as a new "advanced architecture" related to the extreme operativization – both virtual and real – of the new technologies and the assumption of a multiple and as such more complex space-time-information, definitively linked to what has come to be known as the "digital universe".

This will be an architecture involved in the conception, organization and design of possible evolutionary systems capable of responding to the challenges of the new informational environment that is already being anticipated: the analysis and strategic reformulation of a city in equilibrium with and within the territory (and not only of its movements and growths, but also of its infrastructures and relational spaces); the definition of a technical development and an intelligent construction

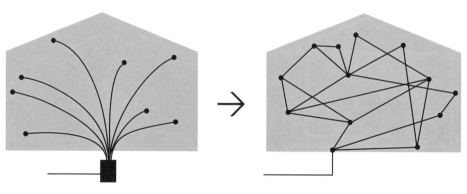

A house with a computer   The house is the computer

capable of interacting effectively with an innovative industry by means of versatile, combinable systems of production; the application of new operative concepts in the design of an "interface-habitat" (of the residential cell and the scenarios – interior and exterior – associated with it); the assumption of the new eco-media and the relation between these and an instrumental approach to the landscape – and to a possible "new nature" – associated with a (paradoxically) more radical because artificial ecology: the new possibilities of programming and computer animation translated into a possible digital "genetics" of form and a possible definition of simulated scenarios, real and virtual, etc.

→ **VERB**   www.iaacat.com

After the objectives and the theoretical framework for the Institute were set up, the students and teachers at the IAAC began by conducting research on a series of questions related to the contemporary domestic environment. How do we live to-day? What is our relationship to the house? What kind of technical structure could a "media house" support? Here we present some of this research, and how it eventually developed into the Media House project itself.

See *The Media House Project* (Barcelona: IAAC / Actar, forthcoming 2004)

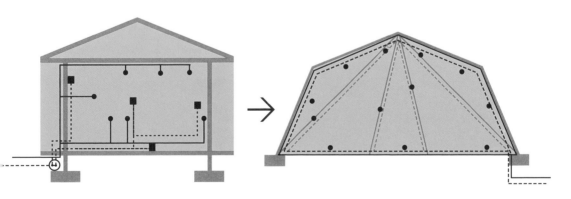

A structure with a network   The structure is the network

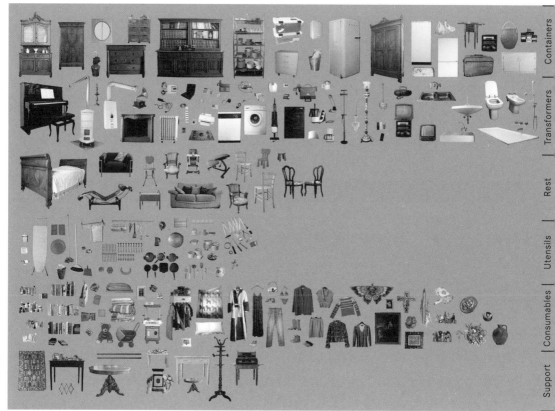

Containers | Transformers | Rest | Utensils | Consumables | Support

"Housing X-Ray", Laura Cantarella > Parameters / Differentials in the interaction with objects and the home: Flexibility and size of the space, cultural components, sex and age of the occupants, style of life, of work (type of activities carried out in the home, visits, presence of professional activity in the home, amount of time spent at home) presence of children, relation with outside space (extrovert / introvert), length and type of possession (ownership / rent), presence of other types of living beings (plants, animals), location in relation to the city (historic centre, residential neighbourhood, around outside of the city) presence of non-family members, presence of connections (phone, television, internet).

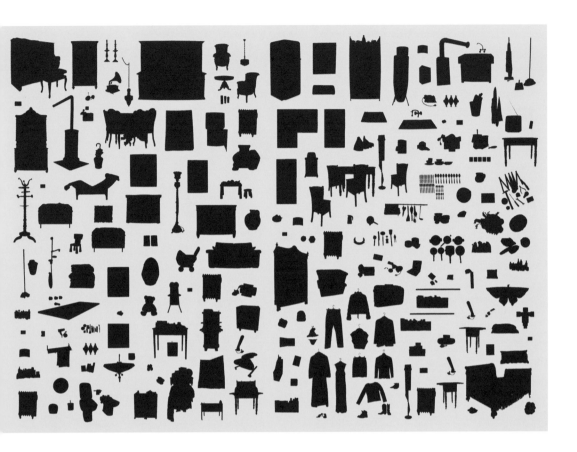

Is the house a laboratory?

Can appliances communicate
with children?

Can the bed be configured
as a tool for eating?

Are there differences between spaces
for children and for adults?

Prototype development > Maurizzio Bonicci, Giovanni Franceschelli
and Silvia Banchini

Local area networks: Megabus, Ring, Star > The challenge of a Media House
structural project is to conceive the technology; that is, to develop an electronic and
digital infrastructure which is the structure itself. Using steel and aluminium profiles,
a section adapted to house the wiring can be drawn. These profiles, which have
structural properties, are equipped with a plug system which permits all types of
access. With this infrastructure it would be possible to configure a structurally stable
but electronically flexible Media House.

MEGABUS The first project is represented by the spiral of a new DNA that envelopes,
stimulates and puts the human being in contact with his surroundings, both exterior
and interior. This spiral describes a free, continuous space open to any configuration,
like an infinite thread that is extendible and reproducible and adapts to all situations.
From the technological point of view, this is represented in a BUS topological system,
where a single wire links interactive hubs which can be added according to needs.
The limit of the space described by this system is represented by an active
wrapping, designed to record and provoke interactions with the human being. But
the development of the electrical circuit in this open but linear system gave rise to
problems at several levels. From a technical point of view, the BUS system can suffer
an unforeseen breakdown if it cuts out at some point. Moreover, failure at one access
point in the BUS system could affect the other points, unless they are designed to
shut down when this happens.

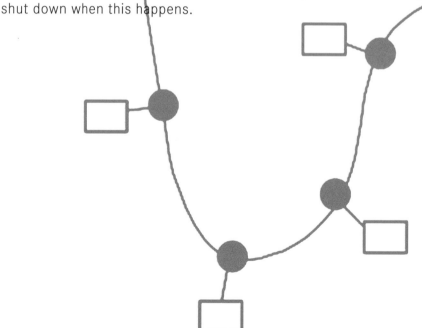

RING, MATTER + INFORMATION To inform means, literally, to "give form", to generate relations among points/moments in a space. Media House is a Data House; it is the place where matter becomes information/communication, where non-matter is movement. The former receives and translates, the latter offers spatial configurations

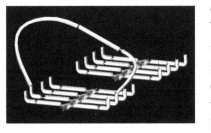

of temporary intervals which go on uninterrupted. To conceive the fusion of structure + infrastructure + skin perhaps means to conceive a system able to be at once structural box and interactive surface, configured to listen to and move with man. Following the first step – in which the space of the house is defined by a linear structural element designed to carry in its interior the entire infrastructural network, with equal density at any point – the idea emerges of being able to define active and inactive spatial fields with different infrastructural data. If we compare this with the bone structure of the human being, the house has a physical and media support in a spinal column, through which run the supply networks (macronet + micronet) with "ribs" attached. Each rib distributes energy and information, and some also distribute air, water, gas, etc. with the aim of preparing the space for use in a given moment, according to needs. The skin connected to the skeleton receives information from the micronet, reacts, produces and modifies its characteristics according to the processes of change which occur in the exterior/interior of the house. The space is thus configured as a platform of events, a composition of increasingly different independent units, portions that contract and dilate, mix and merge. The idea gains strength in the possibility of "switching a space on and off", in the will to read the relation of the person with his surroundings as a temporary reoccupation of an unmarked space.

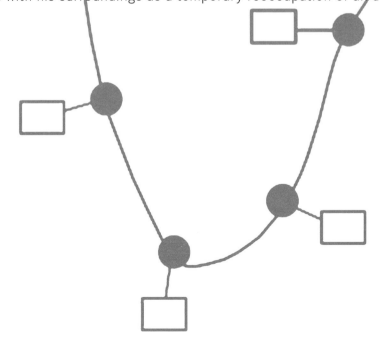

STAR, STRUCTURE AND RELATIONS Investigating the relations that mediate between an event and the time in which the latter manifests itself, we have come to define the concept of movement as a key factor in the generation of new spatiality.
The space dilates, shrinks and modifies over time. On the other hand, events, in manifesting themselves, are able to produce instantaneous complex spatial organizations. Therefore, the space is the fruit of a symbiotic process between two terms; that is, events and time. The mutability and the instantaneousness of these phenomena generate relational spaces and spaces for confrontation, representable through informal, non-conventional geometries, which emerge from either sensorial perceptions or the study and processing of the information. Thus, architecture adopts a new life and, as in nature, the organizational complexity of life does not follow programmes; in informational space and field subject to turbulences specific, structures able to originate endless abstract configurations are generated.
The space, comprising material structures and atoms, can no longer be understood only as relations in metric or anthropometrical dimensions, but rather is identifiable in social, psychological and sensorial dimensions. We need ever more reactive fields or surfaces that provoke tactile, olfactory, visible and auditory sensations; that is, sensations that allow us to enter projective spaces, where perceptions and stimuli continue to mix. Accordingly, "idea" and "imagination" follow the same route, nearly merging in one, allowing us to conceptualise that which we can or cannot see "...of plastic art, architecture becomes life engineering..." Our investigation concludes in the space, with incursions in various directions, processing data and converting it into information, in order to concretise it in the imaginary of technological references obtained through reticular spatial structures composed of lines and nodes.
The reversibility of such structures can assume unprecedented geometries and unpredictable spatial configurations, as well as bearing informational genes.
A reticular structure, projected from an atomic point of view, is prepared to house a local area network (LAN) which can read and recombine all the bits of information

present both inside and outside the space. In this case, the structural node also becomes an "effective point" because it is able to house microchips, sensors and servers, while the poles become "conductors" of wires, fibre optics and electricity. Following this principle, the LAN draws a stellar topology, whose structure becomes a modifying organism of spaces and producer of new relations. The macrostructure and the microinfrastructure appear and disappear, creating areas of high and low density of weft. In this sense, the house is no longer an object, but rather a place of infinite relations among objects, able to process information to the point of creating a multiplicity of realms. An apparent chaos, a realm without rules, a landscape without instructions, all ready for immediate occupation. An active matrix, equipped with an interface able to detect diverse agents in order to create reactive spatial geographies, where in the end the technological structure disappears, ceding its place to the relational structure. As in the human body, the bone, muscle, blood and brain structures intersect, giving life to an organism; architecture, constructed matter and technological support join in a conscious confusion. This investigation into the theme of the structure, which tends towards a "stellar" system, modifies the "house" concept, passing from corporeal (inert matter) to incorporeal (living matter). A shift towards tools of speed, means of transport and aspects of new nature.

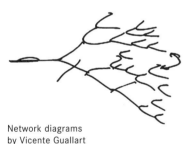

Network diagrams
by Vicente Guallart

Media House program > 'In order to develop "the house", which includes both the design of spaces and objects and the development of software, 22 different layers were defined. The people responsible for supervising these layers set out to define specific areas of development with the potential to take on a life of their own beyond the "Media House."

SPACE

1. **World=City-House** > If the home is a place for work, leisure, shopping and rest, is the house a microcity? How do we design a multifunctional house? How do natural, artificial and digital spaces interact?
2. **Data Use House** > How can a house be designed to ensure a total flexibility of uses?
3. **Teleworking** > Where do people telework? How do people telework? Is there a specific space for this?
4. **Play Place** > If the house is a place for leisure, how do we play at "1:1 scale"?
5. **Car Room** > Is the car another space of the house, connected to it and its environment? How do the streets respond to intelligent cars?
6. **Chroma Room** > Does the house have a space for immersive video-conferencing? Is there commercial exploitation of virtual spaces?
7. **Media Kitchen** > How does a kitchen have to be for us to learn from it? What knowledge do we generate when we cook and eat?
8. **Landscreens** > Does the house have virtual windows in the form of natural or artificial landscapes?
9. **Ergonomics** > How is information ergonomics integrated as physical ergonomics?

TECHNOLOGY

10. **Filament (Media Lab)** > Can all of the objects be connected to one another, without a hierarchy? Is the house a computer?
11. **Human House Interface** > Through what interfaces do we relate to "intelligent houses"? How do we control the flows of information between the physical world and the digital world?
12. **Wired House** > How does information reach objects and spaces? What new wiring does the house incorporate?
13. **Intelligent objects** > What are intelligent objects or furniture like? Are they physical icons of their digital behaviour?
14. **Artificial Intelligence: House to House (H2H)** > How does a house think? How does the house incorporate machine learning algorithms? How does one house relate to another?
15. **Sustainable House** > How much energy does a re-informed house consume? What systems of recycling does it use?
16. **Reactive Surfaces: IN-OUT** > Can we think of spaces that modify their size in relation to their activity? How do we construct a sensitive surface?
17. **Web House** > What is the Web site of a house? What functions does it perform? Will Web sites be created for the five thousand million houses there are in the world?
18. **Shaping Technology** > Could we think about shaping rather using technology? How to integrate rudimentary personal fabricators in the home?

SOCIETY

19. **Social Internet** > What new social relations does the information society produce? How are time and knowledge shared via the Net? Can buildings share facilities such as Internet access?
20. **Lab Home** > Is the house a laboratory when kids and parents create knowledge?
21. **E-House Administrator** > How is the economic activity of the house managed? What is a digital butler like?
22. **House Database** > How are houses actually built in the global village of today?

STRUCTURE

PROFILE

→ VERB

Following the research, the IAAC began to think of how to materialize it: how to develop both a physical and a virtual structure capable of achieving the flexibility they were aiming for. Here the collaboration with the MIT Media Lab was crucial. H. Shrikumar from MIT says: "In our approach, we take these software components, open the box of hardware, and scatter the software components all over the house. So, even though there is no central computer, the house becomes the computer. An analogy that comes to mind is the old story about milk and sugar. Sugar is sweet, but instead of keeping all the sugar in a box, if you dilute it in a glass of milk, it makes the whole drink that much more enjoyable. Similarly, distributed computing scatters the computer virtually all over the house. You can taste the computer, you can feel the computer, but you can't put a hand on a box and say, this is the "computer." What we have developed at the Media Lab is a way to take many, many small computers, hundreds or thousands even, and tie them virtually to behave like one computer."

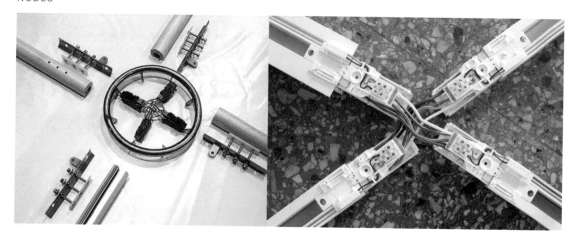

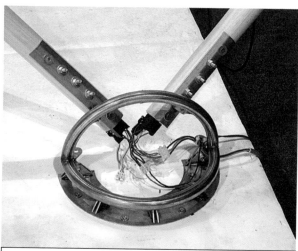

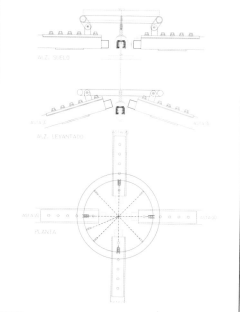

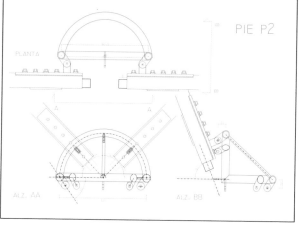

The Media House was finally constructed and presented to the public during the third Metapolis Festival, held in the Mercat de les Flors, Barcelona in September 2001, in parallel with Think Tank, Exhibitions, Performances and the 3rd Metapolis Awards. The project was presented as a staged performance, where different inhabitants "occupied" the house and demonstrated its possibilites.

234

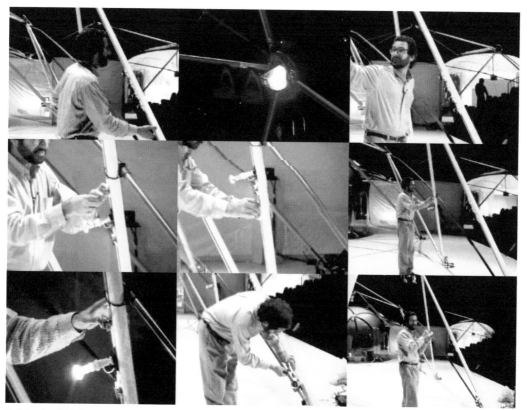

Neil Gershenfeld, from the MIT Media Lab, explaining how the system allows a lightbulb to be plugged in anywhere along the profile.

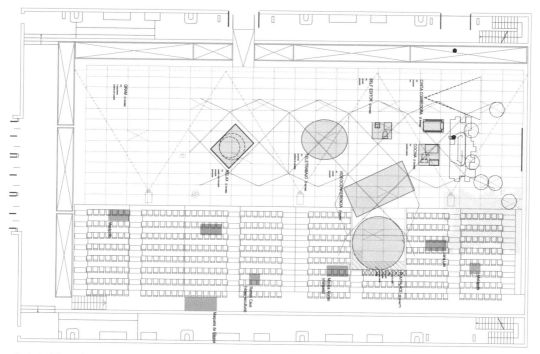

Technical floor plan

Environments. Skin

Dance hall

 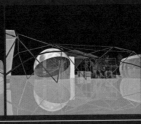  

Relax room

VR Garage

Croma living room

Garden kitchen

Play place

Occupant Joan Palau, dancer

The space you inhabit, that you move, dance or do tai chi in is intelligent and it reads your movement in real time.
Six cameras film the sensors you wear on your body, on your clothes, and they inform the computer of the coordinates x and z. The position of your arms, the movement of your hands, synchronizes with the house. The shutters may lower with your arms, the intensity of the light would follow your rhythm, the house could even record and reproduce your trajectories, your movements, as well as tracking your body.
We create the Motion Track Space.

Occupant Innothna, videogame designers

Space to relax in and for inner knowledge. Employing several interactive tools and manipulating forms, colours, audios and texts the user is led through multiple states of consciousness. The objective is for the user to harmonize his/her inner life and achieve pleasurable and creative sleep.
We create the Cromatherapy room.

Occupant Bert Bongers + Area 3, sensor programmers

 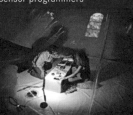

A workshop space, garage, for telework from the home.
A space linked via internet2 to Silicon Graphic high-performance computers.
Million-euro computers become accessible through networked use and become a service offered by companies such as Filmtel. Pixar and DreamWorks computing becomes democratic online and allows you to calculate 3D animations, navigate in VR realms and your "garage" turns into a CAVE.
We create Teleworking Cave.

Occupant Jana Leo, artist

The room in which one lives is in reality the one you spend the least time in. The house is not a place to live in, but for travelling and teleliving. Looking for the next best thing to immediate contact, I use teleconferencing technology to communicate with others. A space that communicates with another space. Your sitting room continues with your grandparents' sitting room. Your meeting, dinner or party is at the same time an extension of another place. Distance is not a problem, families unite and the elderly are not alone.
We create the Space to Space Conference.

Occupant Paco Guzmán, cook

The kitchen is directly connected to a vegetable garden. With hydroponics you can grow crops on vertical surfaces, on a terrace, a balcony, indoors. Sensors control the moisture, climate and watering of the plants. We use the Cultivator planting system and, through internet2, we create new menus, recipes, and exchange information with other kitchens: your family's and the one on TV. We share composting, recycling, the leftover paella and shopping lists with the neighbours.
We create the Kitchen+vertical hydroponic garden.

Occupant family + M. Ángeles García, educational psychologist

We have created a play and learning space for the kids. In the Play Place a family interacts with a space with tactile flooring. They learn and educate their children reproducing together images and sound. We follow the postulates of Glen Doman. We create the Bits play-learning space.

MEDIA HOUSE PROJECT. BARCELONA, SPAIN / MASSACHUSSETS, USA

MIT MEDIA LAB, Massachussets Institute of Technology. <u>Director, Things That Think Consortium:</u> Neil Gershenfeld. <u>Microservers:</u> H. Shrikumar. <u>Interfaces RS 485:</u> Matt Hancher. www.media.mit.edu

FUNDACIÓ POLITÈCNICA DE CATALUNYA. <u>President:</u> Mercè Sala. <u>Director:</u> Miquel Espinosa. <u>Assistant Director:</u> Pau Roig. www.fpc.upc.es

METAPOLIS. <u>Media House Directors:</u> Vicente Guallart, Enric Ruiz-Geli, Willy Müller. <u>Structure:</u> Max Sanjulián. <u>gRAm:</u> Susana Noguero. <u>Structural typologies:</u> Maurizio Bonizzi, Giovanni Franceschelli, Silvia Banchini, Roberto Secchi. <u>Nodes and integration:</u> Michel Oltramare. <u>Housing X-Ray:</u> Laura Cantarella. <u>Furniture concepts:</u> Mekhala Oltramare. <u>I'm a robot:</u> Sophie Cornanguer. <u>Web:</u> Jorge Pasalagua. <u>3D models:</u> Rupert Maurus. <u>Web Interface:</u> AREA3, Federico Joselevich, Chema Lungobardo, Sebastián Puiggros, Elisa Lee, Manel Ruiz. <u>Data visualization:</u> innothna, Julio Hardisson, Daniel Bravo, Carles Ballvé. <u>Lighting:</u> Toni Rueda.

<u>Project consultants:</u> Robert Brufau, architect; Jaume Arderiu, architect; Ramon Sanguesa, UPC; Bert Bongers; Paco Guzmán, kitchen and garden; Mónica Alonso, chromotherapy; Jana Leo, videoconferencing.

<u>President of Metapolis:</u> Manuel Gausa. <u>Metapolis Research Meeting graphics:</u> Ramon Prat. <u>Discussion moderator:</u> Xavier Costa. <u>Directors of the Advanced Architecture and Digital Cities postgraduate course:</u> Vicente Guallart, Artur Serra, Manuel Gausa. www.metapolis.com

ELISAVA. <u>Director of the Interfaces masters course:</u> Núria Díaz. <u>Play Place:</u> Jaime Colom. <u>New baby:</u> Karina Cocho. <u>New kid:</u> Marina Turró. <u>Web house:</u> Fabiola López , Joao Esteves, Marta Pimienta. <u>Humanhouse interface:</u> Enric Gili. <u>Media kitchen:</u> Marcos González, Susana Juan. <u>Self editor:</u> Yoel Lenti. <u>Chromaroom:</u> Ignacio Mondine, Miguel Sola <u>Chromotherapy:</u> Estela Ocampo.

<u>Project tutors:</u> M. Ángeles Garcia, psychologist; Jose Manuel Berenguer, Orquesta del Caos; Sergi Jordà, UPF; Carlos Silva, TechnoMedia; Sergio Schvarstein, MM Factory. www.iccic.edu/elisava

I2CAT,Internet 2 a Catalunya. Sebastiá Sallent, director; Artur Serra, Rosa María Martín, Anna Agustí, Josep Paradells, UPC; Josep Prous, Prous Science; Jesús Alcober, Cristina Cervelló, Josep Mangues, UPC; Jesús Salillas, Prous Science; Pablo López, Hospital de Sant Pau. www.i2-cat.net

DAEL, Dave Witter; Expaces, Leo Grebot; Hector Milla, Mediapark; Gonçal Bonhomme, Al-pi Comunicacions; Mariano Lamarca, MENTA; Xavier Kierschner, Nortel Networks.

Metapolis Research Meeting Production: <u>Metápolis coordination:</u> Marine Budin, Lídia Gilabert. <u>Photography:</u> Laura Cantarella, Luís Ros. <u>Video:</u> Marko. <u>Brochure design:</u> Eloi Ortuño. <u>Plan Mercat de les Flors:</u> Carolina Sanza, Jordi Fernández. <u>Technical assistance:</u> Pilar Gasque, Laura Jiménez, Barbara Oelbrandt, Christine Bleicher, Li An Tsien. <u>Performance coordination:</u> Carles Poy. <u>Technical coordination:</u> Carlos Silva. <u>Audiovisual installation:</u> BAF. <u>Set construction:</u> Manterola. <u>Plastics:</u> Insolplast. <u>Profiles:</u> Diorama. <u>Garden:</u> Burés. <u>Hydroponic watering:</u> Regaber. <u>Motion Tracking:</u> System. <u>Videoconference:</u> Techno Trends. <u>Lighting equipment:</u> Iguzzini.

In 1701, a galley slave escaped from the military prison of Valencia. Following weeks of desperate flight, he found refuge in a remote mountain village, on the northern frontier of the kingdom. Now living as shepherd, he made his home in a ramshackle barn. Two years after his arrival, with his own hands and the power of an old mule, he rebuilt the barn, and thus was born the humble dwelling that was to be the hiding-place for his secret. Summers would find him sitting outside awaiting the flight of the crying swallows, trying to put out

Lles, Catalonia

of his mind the possibility of the fateful day when the authorities might come after him. The escaped convict died in 1711, leaving no family. In 1796, the stones of the house, now empty and derelict, were used to raise by a stream the forge and abode of family who had moved up from the valley. On the stone lintel of "Cal Ferrer" – the blacksmith's house – was carved the date 1801. In 1950, the last of several generations of blacksmiths closed the forge due to lack of business.

House in Lles > Arturo Frediani

Arturo Frediani > In 1997, my wife and I, carrying our four-month-old son Marco, took a hike in the Pyrenees. We were crossing a small village when we stopped to drink from the fountain, enjoy the views and rest in front of an old blacksmith's shop.

It wasn't until Marco had turned three that I heard about the place again. Some clients told me about a possible site for their second residence, coincidentally located in the same village. The same ruin. The same mountains: romantic fate[1]. In November 2000, the scattered stones began to raise new walls. Two hundred years after it had been inscribed, the original lintel was moved to its present location at the base of the fireplace.

After that surprising first contact, we set down to study the building code for the area, to see what it had to say. From the outset, we wanted to move the discussion beyond the issues that obsessed the authors of the document, thus avoiding confrontation with the generic formal elements to clear the way for our equations of compatibility. From the outset, we sought above all to carefully superpose our proposal over the old story. As the galley slave had done, we sought our independence at the margins.

The building regulations focused on retaining material appearance. Most of the new projects in the valley follow construction methods in which the materials play a merely justificatory role. While we contemplated warily the most specific paragraphs regarding the obligatory introduction of such-and-such elements under such-and-such circumstances, we were not at all opposed to the use and extensive application of the materials with which the village had originally been built: wood, tile and stone. The only condition we insisted on was that they would always be subject to a direct use, whether technological or primitive.

Those walls of the original house that remained standing were incorporated into the project. In both these walls and those that would have to be raised, the stone would conserve its good 70cm of thickness and self-supporting capacity.

The steel structure and the wood framework on the façades and interiors would be inspired by the constructional principle of a Steinway & Sons grand piano. In the 19th century, the introduction of a cast-iron plate gave the instrument a clearer, more sustained tone, while it also stayed in tune longer. Our idea was that the steel structure would similarly maintain the dimensional stability of the wooden framing as the aging process of the building advanced. We liked thinking about a process that had already lasted years. In the insertion of new layers, we tried to identify the elements of the system that could be processed in a contemporary and unbiased manner. We wanted to avoid at all costs any nostalgic reconstruction. You could neither compare the present life in the village with that which had laid out its streets, nor compare the way the new residents spent their weekends with the original subsistence economy.

To begin with, we took physical samples of primitive growth tissue. These samples were to be grown in vitro and subsequently expanded and cut to fit the project: units of sloped roof, the simplest one we could find in the village, reproduced as fractals. Unfinished, unvarnished wood surfaces, many of them no longer in existence and discovered in old photos.

The different volumes with a shed roof were adjusted next to one another around the threshing floor. Obviously, the steel bearing structure would have fewer limitations than the primitive walls. This would prove to be something of an oxymoron in the 6m span in the main room. The wood of the façade was to be laid out in a continuous five-sided polyhedron. The windows and accesses were to appear in the breaking of the lathed planes and would then disappear ritually before abandoning the house. The interiors reveal an unusual programme, surprising in this project, with a process of mitosis or cellular division. The floor plan, figure-8 shaped, has two sectors communicated by a 2m-wide passage. The main sector is a complete dwelling, containing the main bedroom. The other sector could be made into an independent dwelling if it were fitted with a kitchen. By being separate, their respective stairways allow for independent access to the upper floor.

In addition to the conventional rooms, there is a secret space, the only one that does not open out on to the threshing floor. We shall only say that it exists. Neither its purpose, nor its form, nor its location within the project concern the reader.

1. See Denis Diderot, *Jacques le fataliste et son maître.*
   Paris: Gallimard, 1977; Paris: Flammarion, 1997.

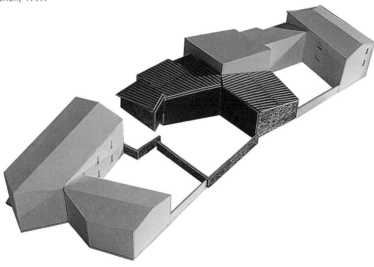

Joaquín Pérez > I experienced the birth of the project of the house in Lles. What I remember most are those first little models that Arturo made, and above all, how he did them. First he would draw simultaneously all the different parts of the model. Then he would cut out the pieces, again all at the same time. Then he would fold the pieces. And finally he would fit the pieces together and glue them in place. There was never any possibility of turning back, corrections or modifications as the process advanced. It was a pre-planned, serial construction. In the last of those little models, the pieces were cut from photocopies of the textures of the materials (stone, ceramic tile, wood) that were to be used in the work.

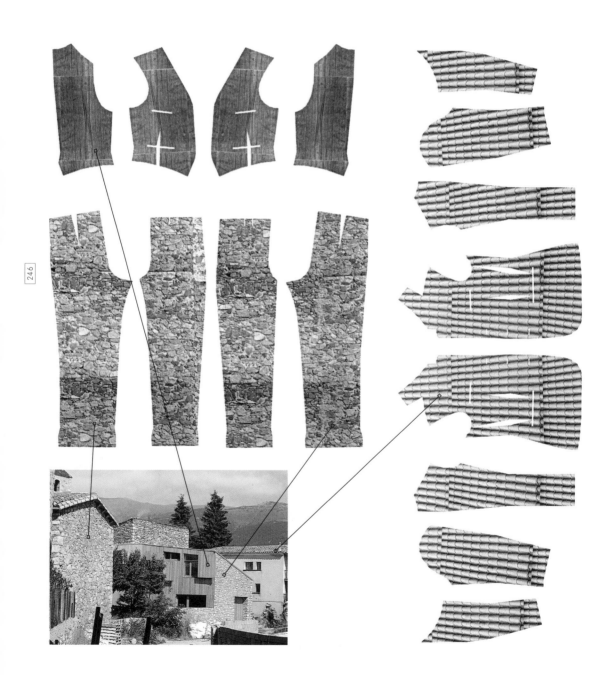

He successively folded these "bits of material" like wrapping, partially delimiting different spaces, spaces which would be defined in their final assembly. For those of us present at the time, the process was more of a game, a puzzle to which only Arturo held the key (try as we would, we never figured out how the pieces fitted together).

Now, as you move about the recently finished house, you can re-experience those surfaces. Feel how their different textures, colours, sounds, even smells surround you. The same enveloping sensations you experience when trying on new clothes. A house conceived like a suit, made-to-fit.

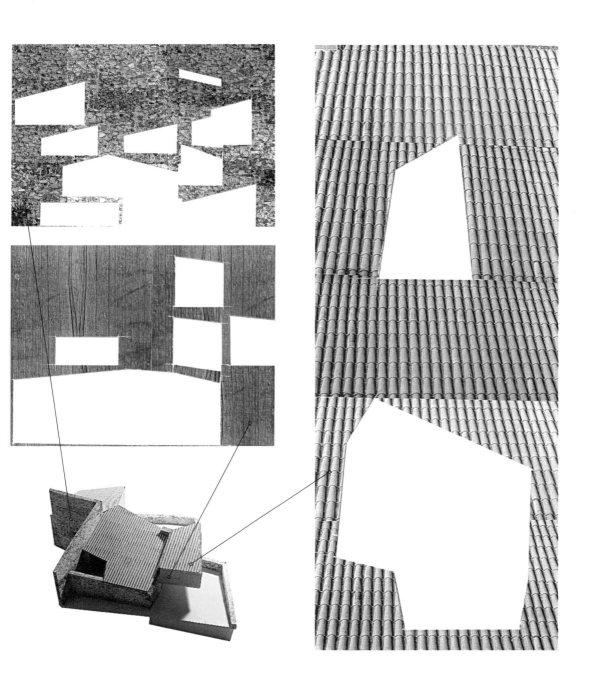

HISTORY OF A SHUTTER (A PARTIALLY FOLD-OUT FAÇADE) While traditionally in houses in La Cerdanya (this region of the Pyrenees) openings are small, rarely greater than 1.2m in width, the code that dictated the inclusion of shutters nowhere limited the size of the openings on the south-facing façades. Fortunately, nor did the code specify how such elements should open; it was assumed that they would swing out.

The location of the openings on the façade of the house was to depend exclusively on the internal organisation of the space and on their maximum size. The façade was drawn according to the sweep of the shutters. Half of the south-facing ground floor façade would be open, with apertures of greater than three meters in width. The other half would be reserved for the shutters when they were opened. The dimensions of the shutters and other windows on the first floor posed from the outset major problems for construction within the traditional system.

Thus, the client's demands depended on the applicability of a system able to provide for easy manual movement of shutters the size of a fair stretch of wall.

At first, in order to achieve precise fitting to the planes of the façade, we worked on a sliding system used in the automotive industry for van doors. Specifically, the hardware on the *Ford Transit* seemed to be the most adaptable to the project. Later, however, we arrived at the conclusion that, in high-altitude conditions, the bearings might well freeze up in the cold.

Having discarded the ready-made, industrial solution, we set our sights on the development of a self-tech mechanism that would meet our specifications. Shutters of up to 7m^2 in size and weighing 130kg had to be easy to open and completely manual in operation. The relation with the interiors, open-closed positions, and the maximum size of the shutters themselves would determine the design of the façades.

Now taking our inspiration from the doors on city buses, we created *ex-novo* a system of laterally-sliding shutters, using – in contrast with the bus doors – a mechanism without guides and with two swing arms instead of just one. The shutters were hung from two points and balanced by a third. In a workshop we worked with a 0.35m^2 prototype with a 40cm arm until we obtained satisfactory performance. We then did a test at real scale, multiplying the overall size by twenty and the arm by four.

HOUSE IN LLES, CATALONIA. SPAIN

Client: Xavier Garriga, Conxita Poch. Architect: Arturo Frediani. Collaborator: Francesc Oller. Engineer: Static Engineering, Barcelona. Surveyor: Mercè Martín Valls, Cerdanyola del Vallès. Contractor: Construccions i Restauracions Peypoch, Castellar de n'Hug. Carpentry: Fusteria "El Pí", Bagà. Structure and metalwork: Buscall, Berga. Cost: 312,500 euros. Start of work: September 2000. End of work: June 2002. Cerdanya rural building, subzone 4b typology, aligned with road. Lot area: 361.39 m^2 (min. = 200 m^2). Floor area ratio: 0.95:1 (343.32 m^2). Occupation of the site relative to total lot area: 30%-60% (min. 102.99, max. 205.99 m^2). Max. number of floors: Ground floor +1. Height above street level: 5.70 m above the slope of the road.

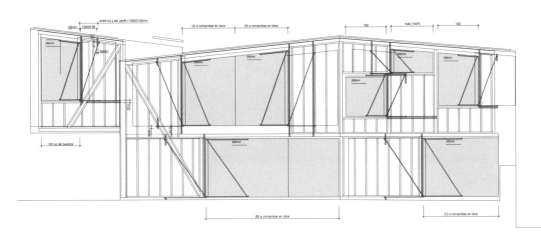

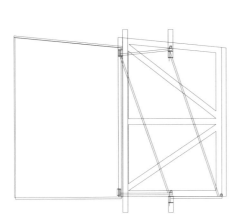
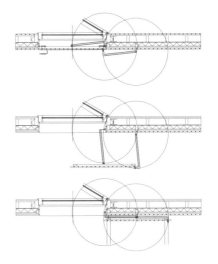

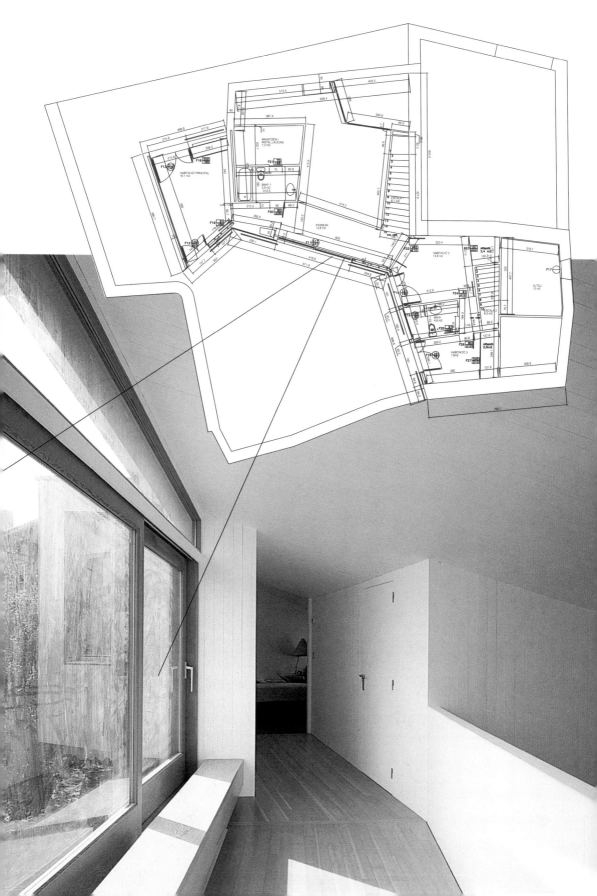

Matsunoyama, Niigata
160 minutes from Tokyo

258

MATSUNOYAMA

TOKYO

Matsunoyama Natural Science Museum > Takaharu & Yui Tezuka Architects / MIAS

HEAVY SNOW The Matsunoyama Natural Science Museum stands in the middle of a mountain in Niigata, famous for its very heavy snowfall: 5 meters cover on average, up to 30 meters per year. There is so much snow that the roots of the beech trees in the nearby forest are inclined downward on the hillside from the weight of the snowfall each winter.

The museum serves as an educational facility for natural science, holding exhibitions on a range of natural phenomena and inviting scientists-in-residence to conduct investigations. It opened as an artwork during the Echigo-Tsumari Art Triennale in 2003, with the collaboration of various artists.

View from the other side of the valley

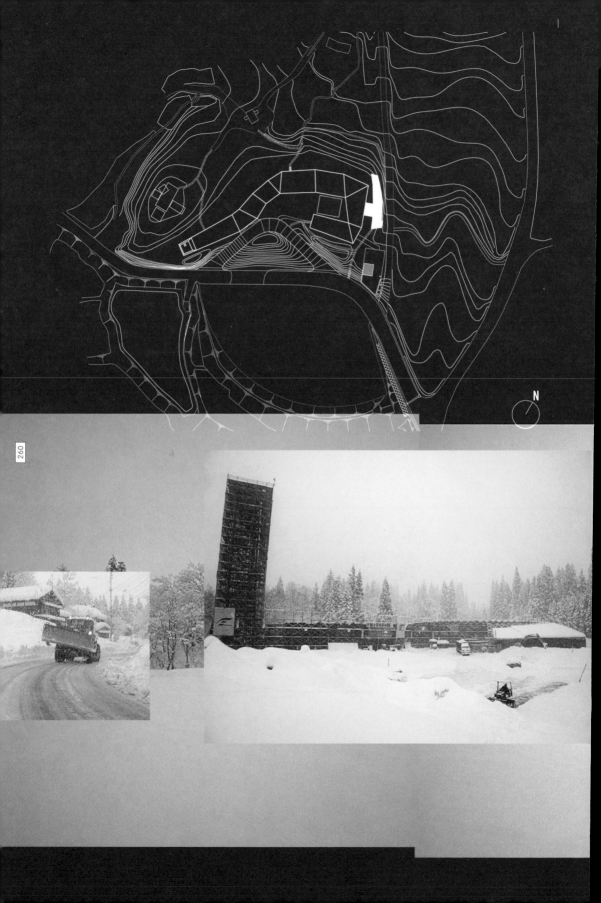

IRON SNAKE For this climate condition, the building is made of 6mm welded Corten steel plates. The whole building is 160m long, and contracts up to 20cm with the cold in winter. The structure functions like that of a submarine, bearing the burden and pressure of 2000 tons of heavy snow (1.5 tons/m^2). For reasons of resistance the windows are made of thick acrylic plates instead of glass with frames, allowing viewers to see natural lifeforms and light filtering through sections of the snow, like in an aquarium. The biggest window is 14.5m x 4m and weighs 4 tons.

SEE-THROUGH This museum is designed to show the environment around rather than the space inside. Thanks to the big acrylic windows, with a 98% transparency and no frames, it seems that there is nothing between inside and outside. The building has the form of an open tube, with windows at the corners and ends of every space so that there are always openings behind and ahead of you.

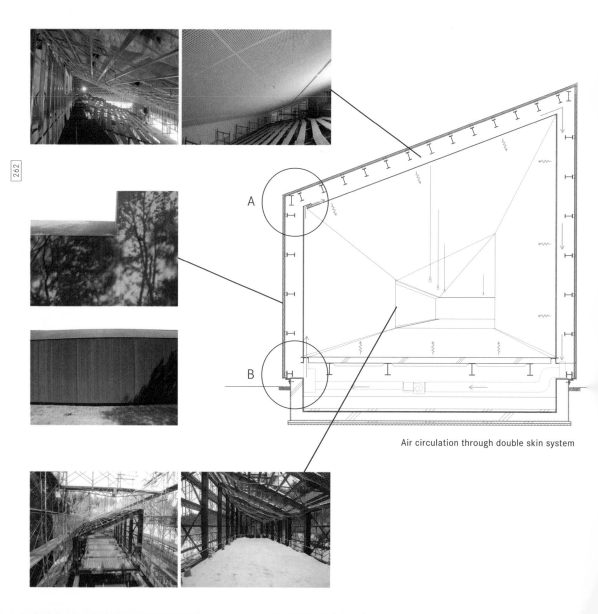

Air circulation through double skin system

SECTION DETAIL

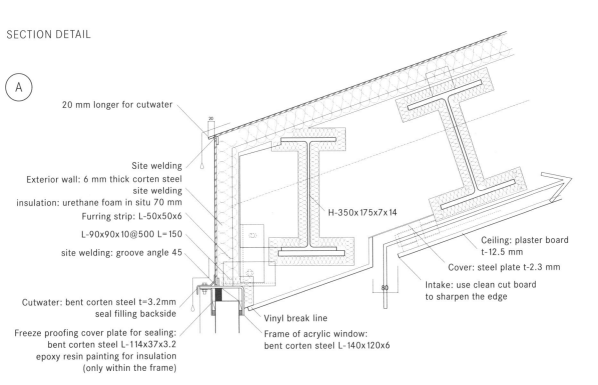

A

20 mm longer for cutwater

Site welding

Exterior wall: 6 mm thick corten steel
site welding
insulation: urethane foam in situ 70 mm
Furring strip: L-50x50x6
L-90x90x10@500 L=150
site welding: groove angle 45

H-350x175x7x14

Ceiling: plaster board
t-12.5 mm

Cover: steel plate t-2.3 mm

Intake: use clean cut board
to sharpen the edge

Cutwater: bent corten steel t=3.2mm
seal filling backside

Freeze proofing cover plate for sealing:
bent corten steel L-114x37x3.2
epoxy resin painting for insulation
(only within the frame)

Vinyl break line

Frame of acrylic window:
bent corten steel L-140x120x6

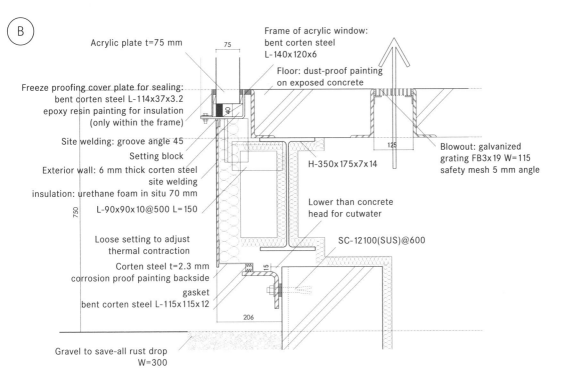

B

Acrylic plate t=75 mm

Frame of acrylic window:
bent corten steel
L-140x120x6

Floor: dust-proof painting
on exposed concrete

Freeze proofing cover plate for sealing:
bent corten steel L-114x37x3.2
epoxy resin painting for insulation
(only within the frame)

Site welding: groove angle 45

Setting block

Exterior wall: 6 mm thick corten steel
site welding
insulation: urethane foam in situ 70 mm
L-90x90x10@500 L=150

H-350x175x7x14

Blowout: galvanized
grating FB3x19 W=115
safety mesh 5 mm angle

Lower than concrete
head for cutwater

SC-12100(SUS)@600

Loose setting to adjust
thermal contraction

Corten steel t=2.3 mm
corrosion proof painting backside
gasket
bent corten steel L-115x115x12

Gravel to save-all rust drop
W=300

Takaharu Tezuka   Yui Tezuka

1. Tokyo office

4. Concrete foundation

5. Office on site

8. Steel frames on site

9. View from the observatory tower

12. Playing on site

13. Finishing

2. Competition phase model

3. Name cards

6. Meeting with clients

7. Assembly in factory

10. View from the tower (snowy day)

11. Carrying acrylic window

14. Finished

15. 1000 people came to the opening

FOUNDATION MOVEMENT The Corten steel skin expands and contracts according to differences in temperature, the 160m length of the building varying by up to 20cm. To absorb this change, the building is loosely fixed to the foundations, to allow and control this movement.

Base plate

Loose hole allows sliding in one
direction (parallel to A8 axis)

Loose joint to absorb the
movement of the building

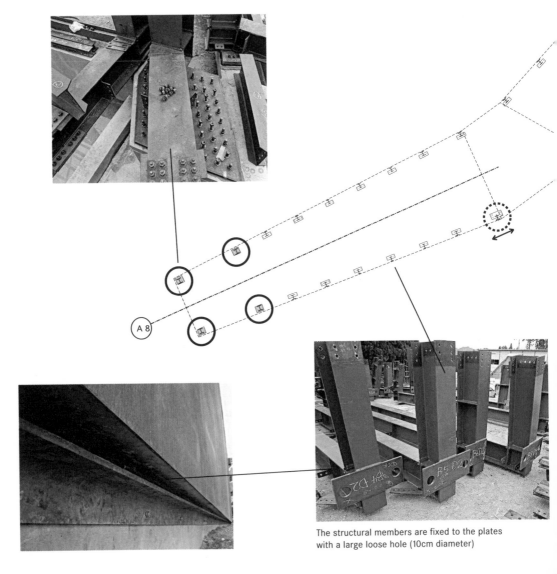

A 8

The structural members are fixed to the plates
with a large loose hole (10cm diameter)

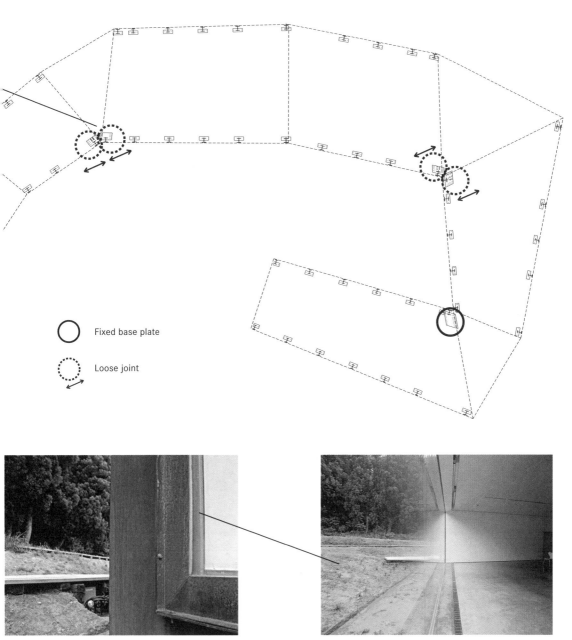

Architects: Takaharu & Yui Tezuka Architects / MIAS cost: 756,000,000 yens. Area: site area 4269,15 m², building area 997,45 m², total floor area 1248,18 m², building height 33,49 m. Competition: 2000, design phase: 2001-2002, construction: 2002-2003, completion 2003.

○ Fixed base plate

◌ Loose joint

To absorb the expansion and contraction of the steel skin, the frame of acrylic window is 4cm wide

Acrylic window without support frame

FIRST FLOOR PLAN

Observatory tower

View from the observatory tower

The tower has two works of art: LED screens which react to cosmic rays by Takuro Osaka, and sound work for sump water by Taiko Shono

268

View from the tower

Entrance

Exhibition room

The parking lot is the work of the artist Tadashi Kawamata

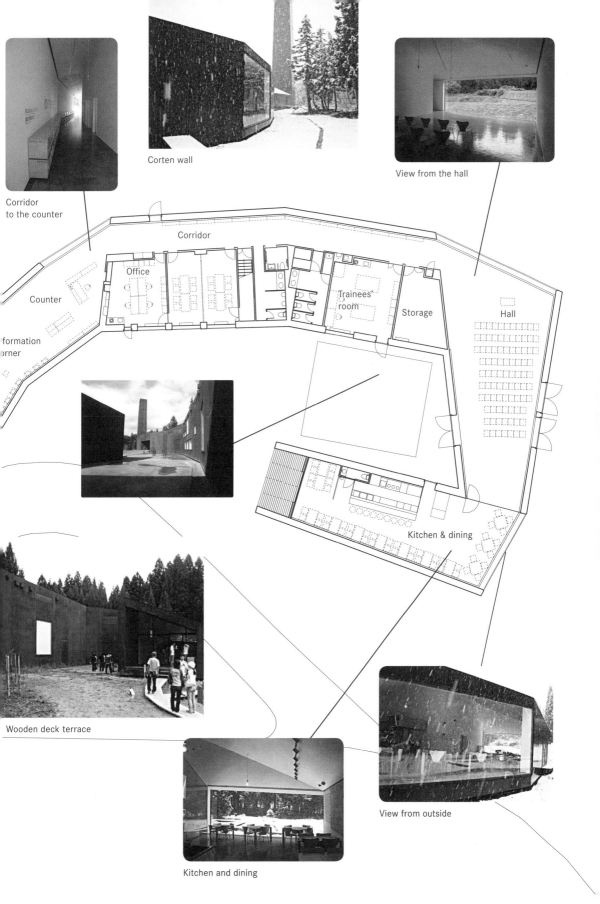

Corridor
to the counter

Corten wall

View from the hall

Corridor

Office

Counter

Trainees'
room

Storage

Hall

formation
orner

Kitchen & dining

Wooden deck terrace

Kitchen and dining

View from outside

LONG-TERM USE The Corten skin ages well over time, generating beautiful stripes in reaction to rain and snow. During the long winter, the building is completely buried in the snow except for the observation tower, like a big snake rearing up to see the valley of Matsunoyama. The surrounding landscape is designed to revive the ancient beech forest that used to populate the site.

© Katsuhisa Kida

Hadano
1 hour 40 min. southwest of Tokyo

Roof House > Takaharu & Yui Tezuka Architects / MIAS

The Takahashis used to live in a very ordinary Japanese-style house with a steep, tiled roof. They liked climbing onto the roof as often as they could to enjoy a meal or to relax.

When they commissioned their new house, their first request was that the house should have a 'roof to have lunch on.' And that is how the house was built, with a slightly sloping roof that is neither balcony nor terrace, and has no railing...

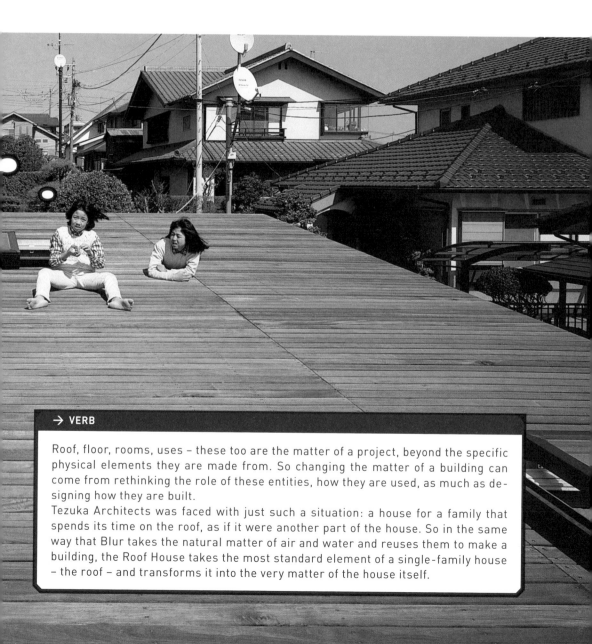

→ **VERB**

Roof, floor, rooms, uses – these too are the matter of a project, beyond the specific physical elements they are made from. So changing the matter of a building can come from rethinking the role of these entities, how they are used, as much as designing how they are built.

Tezuka Architects was faced with just such a situation: a house for a family that spends its time on the roof, as if it were another part of the house. So in the same way that Blur takes the natural matter of air and water and reuses them to make a building, the Roof House takes the most standard element of a single-family house – the roof – and transforms it into the very matter of the house itself.

Architects: Takaharu & Yui Tezuka Architects / MIAS. Site: Hadano, Kanagawa, Japan. Structure: wooden structure on reinforced concrete foundation. Area: site area 298,59 m^2, building area 107,65 m^2, floor area 96.89 m^2. Client: Takahashi family. Cost: 24 500 000 ¥. Construction: Isoda Co., Ltd. Design phase: 03.2000 - 08.2000, construction: 09.2000 - 03.2001. Completion: 2001

276

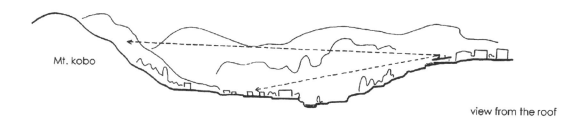

Mt. kobo

view from the roof

The architects, Takaharu and Yui Tezuka, drove us to the house in their old, yellow Citroën 2CV. We were welcomed by the Takahashi family – a couple with two daughters and their grandmother – who kindly accepted our request for a photo session. Through the long design process, the clients had developed a strong relationship with the architects, to the point of treating them as part of the family. We were invited to a delicious meal at the roof table, partly cooked by the Tezukas and partly by the Takahashis, and we enjoyed the views and the spring sun. The site is on the edge of a cliff, and the view from this table opens onto the wide valley and the surrounding mountains, especially Mt. Kobo. It felt like a picnic in the mountains – except for the fact that we could enjoy hot dishes on ceramic plates that came directly out of the kitchen located below the thin roof structure.

Designed with the engineer Masahiro Ikeda, the roof structure is only 15cm thick and is built as a grid system without beams. Thanks to this thinness, the interior spaces of the house and the open-air "room" above are linked without transition spaces. The roof is accessed from several points – from the stairs, from the skylight-windows, or by means of a ladder from any edge of the roof. Even the bathroom has an access skylight and a ladder, so one can climb up to dry out in the sun after taking a shower in the summer.

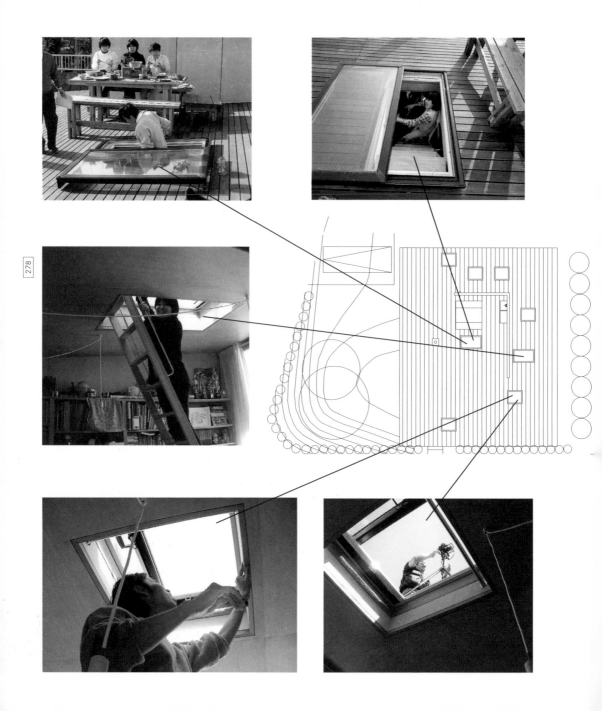

The construction of the roof has a specific connection to some of the other projects in this issue of *Verb*: it is, in fact, the same construction system as the floor slabs of the Mediatheque, designed by the same engineer. But here the reason for this construction is very different: to make the roof as thin as possible so that people can easily climb through it, using the skylights. So the same kind of construction system can find a use in very different buildings, for very different purposes.

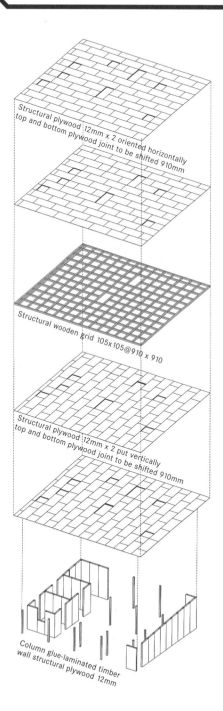

Structural plywood 12mm x 2 oriented horizontally
top and bottom plywood joint to be shifted 910mm

Structural wooden grid 105x105@910 x 910

Structural plywood 12mm x 2 put vertically
top and bottom plywood joint to be shifted 910mm

Column glue-laminated timber
wall structural plywood 12mm

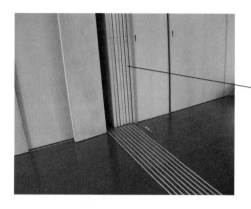

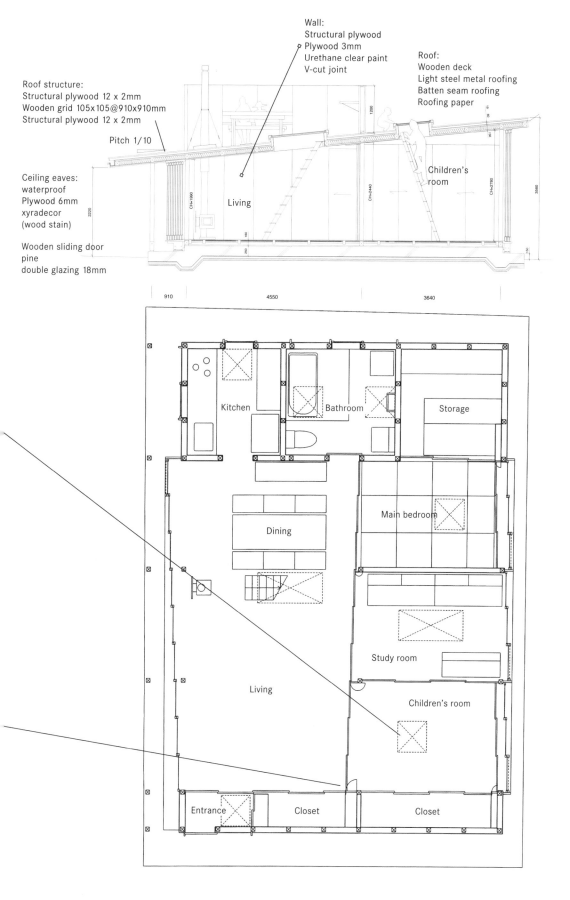

Roof structure:
Structural plywood 12 x 2mm
Wooden grid 105x105@910x910mm
Structural plywood 12 x 2mm

Pitch 1/10

Ceiling eaves:
waterproof
Plywood 6mm
xyradecor
(wood stain)

Wooden sliding door
pine
double glazing 18mm

Wall:
Structural plywood
Plywood 3mm
Urethane clear paint
V-cut joint

Roof:
Wooden deck
Light steel metal roofing
Batten seam roofing
Roofing paper

Living

Children's
room

910   4550   3640

Kitchen

Bathroom

Storage

Dining

Main bedroom

Living

Study room

Children's room

Entrance

Closet

Closet

The interior of the house is a big open space with a separate kitchen and bathroom, which can be subdivided by means of folding partitions according to use. The room includes a Japanese style area for the husband and wife, a study area for the four members of the family, and a children's area, all facing a big living space opening onto the garden.

Each person has his or her own skylight-window that acts as a door to the roof. The furniture and the heating stove were also designed by the Tezukas. The stove, which is enough to heat the whole house, uses small left-over pieces of wood given by the house and furniture builder; in summer, natural ventilation through the house keeps the interior cool without the need for air conditioning.

The garden produces fruit for the family – Kaki and Hassaku citrus – and for their many visitors. There was originally no fence on the site, but so many people came to see the house at all times of the day that a hedge was finally planted.

The 1/10 roof inclination follows the slope of the site, so that the roof becomes a direct projection of the ground. The southern edge of the roof is only 1.9 meters above ground, in order to make it easy for the family to hand over the dishes when they have a barbecue in the garden.

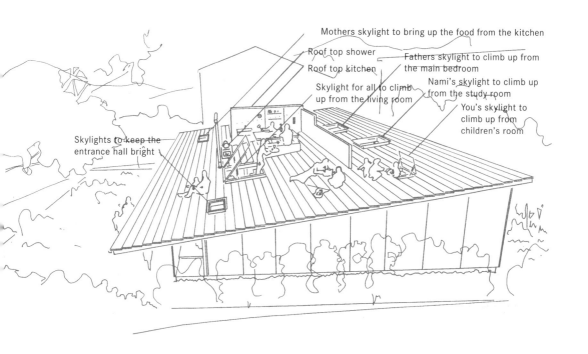

Mothers skylight to bring up the food from the kitchen

Roof top shower

Fathers skylight to climb up from the main bedroom

Roof top kitchen

Skylight for all to climb up from the living room

Nami's skylight to climb up from the study room

You's skylight to climb up from children's room

Skylights to keep the entrance hall bright

We stayed talking and eating – now indoors – until late late at night. On the ceiling, naked light bulbs were plugged in along two lighting rails. When activities moved, the lights followed along. This one-light-for-one-function system was designed by Masahide Kakudate. Although their warm hospitality does not

286

show it, the Takahashis have become the hosts to the many journalists and architecture students who come to visit this house. In this sense the roof house has also changed their lives. This newly acquired fame is for them an enjoyable consequence of the work they did together with the architects in the design of the house.

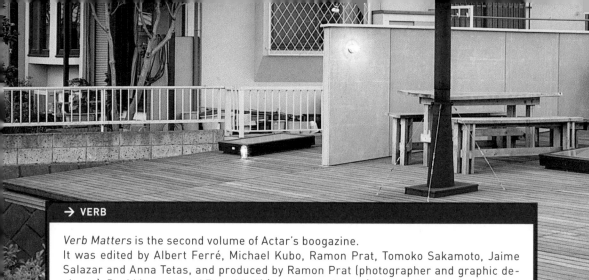

→ VERB

Verb Matters is the second volume of Actar's boogazine.
It was edited by Albert Ferré, Michael Kubo, Ramon Prat, Tomoko Sakamoto, Jaime Salazar and Anna Tetas, and produced by Ramon Prat (photographer and graphic designer), David Lorente and Rosa Lladó (graphic designers), Dolors Soriano (production manager), Oriol Rigat, Carmen Galán and Leandre Linares (scanning and digital production), Edward Krasny, Thomas Daniell and Ian Pepper (translators), and Ingoprint (printing), with the help of Cristina Lladó and Lídia Gilabert (press and public relations), Nicolás Friedmann, Eduard Garcia, Silke Harder, Franck Jamin, Vincent Othats-Dalès, Sanae Tomari and Alejandro Zerené (distribution).
Our thanks to all the authors whose generous contribution of ideas and materials has made this issue possible. In addition, this publication has relied on the invaluable collaboration of Denise Fasanello, Christian Gärtner, Dirk Hebel, Akihira Hirata, Hiromi Hosoya, Eri Ishida, Jan Knikker, Takayuki Miyoshi, Chika Muto, Mariko Nishimura, Kenichi Shinozaki, the Takahashi family (Hiroyuki, Mikiko, Nami, You and Kikuko), Yoshitaka Tanase, Shimpei Tokitsu, Hiroshi Tomikawa, Katrien Vandermarliere, Chris Van Duijn, and Yasutaka Yoshimura.
Photographs: Passera & Pedretti Consulting Engineers (www.ppeng.ch), Dirk Hebel, KDa, Jürgen Mayer H., Takuya Onishi, SANAA, Yasutaka Yoshimura, Toyo Ito & Associates, Architects, Makoto Yokomizo, K.T. Architecture and Hiroshi Tomikawa.

Contact info:
ACTAR
Roca i Batlle 2
E-08023 Barcelona
www.actar.es
phone +34 934 187 759
fax +34 934 186 707
verb@actar-mail.com

Distribution:
info@actar-mail.com

ISBN 84-95273-76-4
DL B-451-2004
Printed and bound in the European Union
Barcelona, January 2004